Outdoor Science Classroom

Easy Lessons & Learning Spaces

by Steve Rich

Illustrations by Tim Foley

Carson-Dellosa Publishing Company, Inc.
Greensboro, North Carolina

Dedicated with love to my son, Spencer Anthony Rich, for helping me
to rediscover the wonders of the outdoors through his eyes
and for making my life an adventure of joy.

As Maya Angelou said, "My son is my monument."

Acknowledgements

In the experiences that led to writing *The Outdoor Science Classroom*, there have been many colleagues who have encouraged me. Foremost among those have been two administrators who are also dear friends. It is with deep gratitude that I acknowledge the unfailing support and outstanding leadership of Carolyn J. Anderson, principal of New Manchester Elementary School, for encouraging my students and me as we built our award-winning outdoor classroom. Carolyn inspired me to be my best and to always take the high road. I also thank the former principal of Chestnut Log Middle School, Jeri F. Mansfield, for seeing potential in me and in our schoolyard, and for trusting me to create my first outdoor classroom. Thank you, also, to the many teachers, students, parents, and community members who helped to make the outdoor classroom a reality.

In creating this book, I must professionally acknowledge the National Science Teachers Association awards program for making the connection to the publisher possible and the board members of the Georgia Science Teachers Association for their encouragement and friendship. Personally, I thank those who have listened to my progress: Glenn Bilanin—for "a little and a lot to ask, an endless and a welcomed task"; Catherine Rich Robinson—for being the very best kind of sister and setting the example of quality teaching; and especially my mother, June C. Rich—the exemplary nurse and outstanding educator, who nursed every injured lizard or snake I found and nurtured my love for the outdoors.

Credits

Author: Steve Rich
Illustrator: Tim Foley
Cover Designer: Peggy Jackson
Editors: Debra Olson Pressnall, Kathryn Wheeler,
and Elizabeth Flikkema
Graphic Layout: Mark Conrad
Cover Photos: © Photodisc; © Digital Vision® Ltd.;
Photo www.comstock.com © 2001 Corbis Corporation;
© 1999 EyeWire, Inc.

ISBN: 1-59441-198-0

Table of Contents

Creating a Space for Learning

Ever look out the window on a nice day and dream about what fun it would be to hold class outside? Your students probably feel the same way! There's a great solution for you and for them: create an outdoor learning laboratory that can be a classroom center for science, math, and language arts lessons.

Teaching outdoors is rewarding for teachers and students alike. And there are many options to creating a classroom-learning lab area outdoors. If you're ambitious and have the resources, you can create an outdoor classroom that you can use from year to year, building and adding to it whenever you're able. But you can also base great lessons on temporary outdoor learning solutions. This book offers suggestions for both alternatives.

To discover how effective outdoor classes can be, go to your curriculum and look at objectives and standards in the areas of life science, earth science, and environmental science. Many of those objectives can be met in simple, inexpensive outdoor lessons—without a field-trip permission slip in sight! This book also offers great math and language arts activities to tie into your curriculum, too.

Multiple reports from around the nation by the State Education and Environment Roundtable show that environment-centered education improves student achievement, builds community partnerships, and even provides an effective context for learning mathematics. Whatever your school's setting—urban, suburban, or rural—there are ways to create an exciting outdoor classroom so your students can participate in the experience.

Getting Started

Your first challenge is to decide whether you want to employ temporary solutions (see page 16) or lay the groundwork for a permanent outdoor learning environment. Either way, it's a good idea to think through the steps in this chapter to help you evaluate your direction.

For a successful outdoor program in which you're creating a more permanent space, you'll need a good garden plan, student/parent/faculty and administrator involvement, and financial support.

Setting up a good plan. Begin by identifying the resources you already have and those you will need. The Schoolyard Inventory chart on page 6 will help you do this. Walk around your school's grounds as you fill out the form. You may be surprised by how many resources you already have in place.

Next, take a look at some plans that have been successfully developed at other schools (see pages 8 through 16). As you look at the plans, pay attention to the components that grab your attention. Which components fit both into your curriculum and your school's site? Which ones could you accomplish with the resources you presently have available? Which ones will let you accomplish your curricular objectives through classes that are interesting to you (since your enthusiasm is critical to student enthusiasm) and fascinating to your students?

Use the elements that you've identified in your screening process as the best ones for your plan. Combine them to draw up your own preliminary plan(s) and get ready to share your vision!

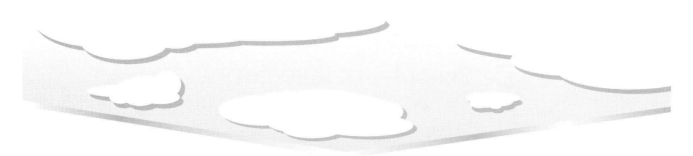

Getting students (and faculty and parents) involved. After you have prepared the inventory and begun planning, give your project a head start on success: show your ideas and information to your school principal and other administrators. You may wish to speak to your students, the faculty, and the PTA or other parent group, too—the more ownership your stakeholders feel, the more they will work toward your outdoor classroom's success. Another way that you can raise the ownership level is to take students on a second inventory survey over the school grounds. They may well be your best advisors in planning the outdoor learning lab; and if they help to plan it, they will want to help maintain it as well.

Another possibility to consider is holding a student contest for outdoor classroom designs. Then see if you can create the images needed to help everyone visualize these ideas. A student or an involved parent who is a good artist might sketch a plan for your schoolyard vision. An art teacher is another great resource—he or she may draw a plan for you or help a student with the plan as part of an art project.

Take all ideas into consideration; then start to fine-tune your plan. Base this tuning on the resources your schoolyard already has, what it needs, and how much funding you expect to get.

Financing the outdoor classroom. Think that you'll never find the money to finance your outdoor learning lab dream? Think again! There is more help available than you might guess. All you need to do is think creatively.

Here are just a few "hidden" resources:
- Master gardeners from the local cooperative extension service are often willing to get involved in planning and establishing school gardens.
- A landscape architect or garden professional might be willing to offer an in-kind donation. Parents might also have skills and business resources to donate.
- The owner of a paving company could donate sand for an archaeological dig area (see page 15).
- A parent or colleague who roots plants in her garden could share some perennials to create a butterfly garden (see page 13).
- A parent who is a chef might like to partner with the school on an herb garden.

You might also consider seeking grant money. As nonprofits, schools are eligible for grants. They also frequently benefit from the donations of charitable individuals and corporations. In Chapter 2, you will find resources and reproducible sample letters to start your funding search. The chapter also offers suggestions for navigating the fund-raising and grant-writing processes.

When your plan is ready, make a final presentation to your principal. Remember to follow proper procedures for approval—many plans have been rejected simply because someone decided not to go through the channels. Have all plans signed and dated by the proper authorities, and be sure to discuss maintenance procedures before beginning your work. This step ensures that you have the resources in place not only to build, but to maintain your outdoor classroom.

Schoolyard Inventory

Take this inventory when you are outdoors and on your school's grounds. Do not try to fill it out from memory because you may miss noting down some valuable resources. Extra lines have been included so that you can add any unique resources that your school grounds offer.

Resource	Available	Feasible	Not Feasible	Estimated Cost
Garden plot				
Mature trees				
Young trees				
Flower containers				
Flower beds				
Semiwooded area for nature trail				
Shaded area				
Group seating				
Area safe from traffic				
Birdbaths				
Butterfly nectar plants				
Butterfly host plants				
Pond or creek				
Patio or asphalt surface for chalk projects				
Access to water/hose				
Access to electricity				

CD-104107 *Outdoor Science Classroom*

Outdoor Classroom Plans, Big and Small

An outdoor learning environment can be as small as one math patio (see page 8) bracketed by two small garden plots. It can be as large as space, resources, and imagination permit. Pages 8 to 12 include plans for successful outdoor classrooms that have been developed at other elementary and middle schools. You'll also find descriptions of patios and different types of gardens in this chapter. Your own outdoor classroom-learning lab can include ideas from these plans as you customize them for your school.

Materials

The plans you'll see on the following pages use many different plants, as well as the following materials. Tips about installation are included to help you consider which materials you may want to use, and what resources you'll need to begin the building process.

Landscape timbers are made of treated lumber, which will last for years outdoors. To secure the timbers to the ground, drill a hole near each end of a timber with a three-quarter inch drill bit. Drive an eight- or ten-inch spike through the timber and into the ground.

Patio blocks come in several colors. Chalk is easiest to see on red or terra cotta blocks. If you're considering another color, buy a sample block and experiment with chalk before making a large purchase.

Before you lay the patio, you will need to level the ground with heavy equipment brought in by a business partner or volunteer. Or you can use the manpower of students, parents, and teachers working together. Use a leveling tool to check the area. You can spread a layer of fine gravel used specifically for the final leveling process, although a patio can be built successfully without it. Putting down dark plastic or weed cloth before installing the blocks will inhibit weed growth through any cracks between patio blocks.

Pathways through outdoor learning spaces are essential to protect plants and other resources. Stepping stones surrounded by non-floating cypress mulch keeps pathways neat and attractive. Avoid pebble pathways—some students may be tempted to throw the pebbles.

Wooden benches are a good choice for seating. If they fall over, wooden benches are less likely than concrete benches to injure children. Plus, they can be built inexpensively. (If you aren't a carpenter yourself, seek a parent or colleague for help in building the benches.) Treated timber often comes in 2 inches x 12 inches x 8 feet lengths that can be cut in half for a bench top. Treated posts can be put into the ground for legs. The finished seating will stand up to student use and the elements and can be repaired with relative ease.

Math Patio Options

A math patio is a central element of an outdoor learning lab environment. It can provide a highly visual way of teaching challenging math concepts. It allows students with different learning styles to see a concrete representation of the idea. A math patio can be created for under $100, but you cannot put a price tag on the value it brings to your math lessons. Here are different types of math patios that you can consider for inclusion in your plan.

A Hundreds Charts Patio is a ten-by-ten grid of concrete blocks (1 foot-square blocks) which allow students to create hundreds charts, graphs, and scale drawings. In the pattern below, the numbers of the hundreds chart have been started. Each square represents a concrete block, and the numbers are written by students with chalk. Although this patio is the larger of the two basic types, it allows greater working space if your plan includes only one patio. *Note:* This patio can double in use as a Calendar Math Patio by simply marking out the desired number of days in a month with chalk. Because each row will have 10 squares, though, the calendar will not look like the standard month representation, which might confuse some students.

S	M	T	W	TH	F	S
					1	2
3	4	5	6	7	8	9
10	11	12	13	14	15	16
17	18	19	20	21	22	23
24/31	25	26	27	28	29	30

A Calendar Math Patio is made of square concrete blocks in a six-by-seven grid to create a standard calendar. You can double the numbers in the last row for the last day or two of the month, a common practice on paper calendars. A calendar patio will be less than half as expensive as a hundreds patio, since it uses far fewer blocks.

In the diagram above, each square represents a concrete block. The letters and numbers would be written by your students. Notice that this set of blocks is laid out in a seven-by-six grid. You need an extra row across the top for the days of the week, and you can have five rows for weeks. Four would work if you need to save money or space.

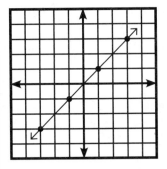

A Math Decicenter or Graphing Patio is a variation of the previous math patios. It is built with larger concrete blocks than the elementary model. Students can use this center when plotting ordered pairs of numbers on a coordinate graph, using chalk to mark and label the grid and location of points. Line and bar graphs can also be created on the math patio.

1	2	3	4	5	6	7	8	9	10

Outdoor Classroom Plans
Elementary Grades

Plan A: Calendar Patio and Two Gardens

An outdoor classroom with one calendar patio and two compact garden plots is well suited for a small area or a limited budget. This plan can easily be expanded later—as the following plans show. You may find that one patio bordered with two garden areas is enough dedicated space for your school and your outdoor teaching plans. In the plan below and the ones that follow, the small gardens are surrounded by landscape timbers.

Even a small garden space can be enhanced with plants to attract butterflies, a birdbath to attract birds, or a variety of plants planted with a theme in mind. See pages 13 through 15 for ideas that will help you select features for this simplest of permanent installations.

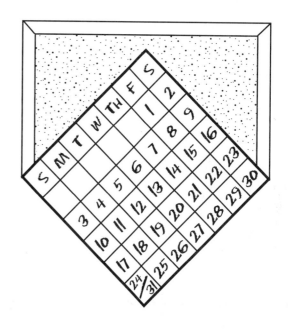

Plan B: Two Patios and Six Garden Areas

If you have success with Plan A, think about a future expansion of your outdoor classroom space. Plan B offers twice as much space as Plan A, with six triangles for gardens. The plan is also flexible. Triangular areas can be turned into gardens or sitting areas. Patios can be created from two calendar grids, two hundreds charts, or one of each. If your school has kindergarten through Grade 5 classes, you can suggest that each grade level be responsible for establishing and maintaining one of the garden areas. Let students plant the gardens as they wish, or discuss with them the various garden ideas presented on pages 13 through 15.

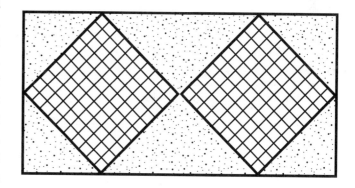

Outdoor Classroom Plans
Elementary Grades

Plan C:
Comprehensive plan for elementary-school outdoor classroom

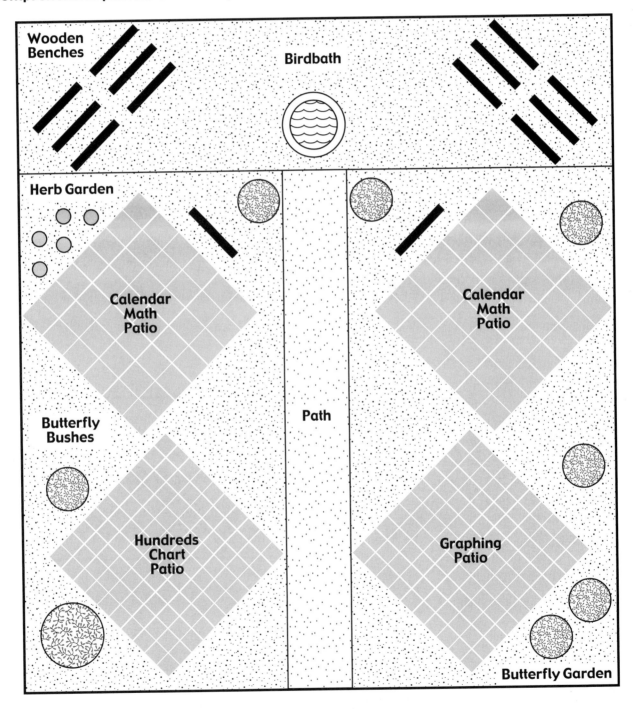

Wooden Benches

Birdbath

Herb Garden

Calendar Math Patio

Calendar Math Patio

Butterfly Bushes

Path

Hundreds Chart Patio

Graphing Patio

Butterfly Garden

Outdoor Classroom Plans
Middle–School Grades

Middle-school students have different learning needs than elementary students. Your outdoor classroom-learning lab design for these students should reflect those needs. For example, consider using larger concrete blocks for your middle school patio. Different colored blocks can help define various work areas for small groups. When planning the garden spaces, choose ones that you think would be most useful to your school and curriculum. For ideas, see the suggestions beginning on page 13.

Plan A: Garden and Two-Color Patio

This simple version of a middle-school plan uses the multi-colored patio blocks described above, and combines them with one of the theme gardens, described on pages 13–15.

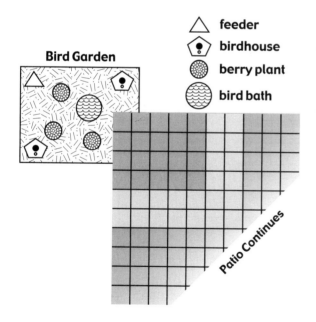

Plan B: Patio and Four Gardens

Another successful plan incorporates four of the garden-activity center ideas from pages 13 through 15. They are grouped around the decicenter or math patio. The patio can serve as the central teaching area, and the gardens frame the learning lab, providing space to study plants, birds, and insects. The archaeological dig area provides great science-social studies crossover opportunities. This design also addresses the need of middle-school students in offering layered possibilities for in-depth lessons. Note that the design shown above provides a perfect separation of activities to support small-group work.

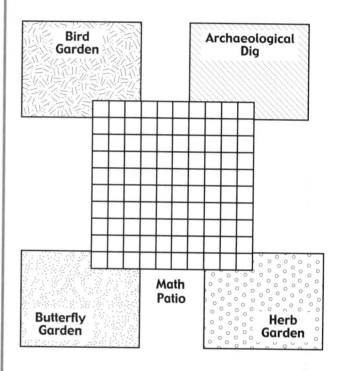

Plan C:
Comprehensive plan for middle–school outdoor classroom

Compost Bins

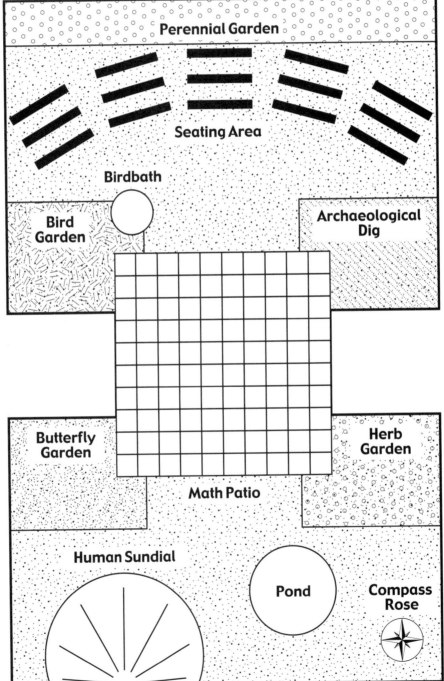

There are many choices to consider for interesting gardens and activity areas. What you select will depend on your curriculum, your resources, and your budget. Then tailor your plan to include the gardens of your choice. Any of the triangular garden areas in the school plans on pages 9 through 12 can be turned into one of the gardens listed below. You may also want to include garden walkways made with stepping stones or patio blocks to make it easier for students to maintain their outdoor learning lab-classroom. In addition to these ideas, be sure to brainstorm with students so that they have input into the final design. And of course, what you plant is determined by what garden zone you live in. Be sure to check gardening books for information about specific plants and whether or not they will flourish in your geographic zone.

Different Kinds of Gardens

Bird Garden. A bird garden attracts birds to your outdoor classroom, and should include food, water, shelter, and a place to raise young. Shelter might be a small tree that your students plant. Food can come from feeders and from natural sources such as berry-yielding plants (blueberries, blackberries) or native grape vines. Purchase a birdbath, or make one by turning a flowerpot upside down and fastening a tray on top. Complete the garden by installing a few birdhouses. Your students will be fascinated as they watch birds lay eggs and raise their young.

Butterfly Garden. Butterflies will visit gardens that provide nectar, caterpillar host-plants, and sunshine. The common butterfly bush, *buddleia*, is hardy and will produce flowers with the nectar butterflies prefer. Most flowers will attract butterflies, but some of their favorites are lantana, marigolds, zinnias, purple-cone flowers, and vinca. Host plants are specific to butterfly species, and females will choose those plants for laying their eggs. Many varieties of Swallowtails prefer cold-hardy parsley, which will grow outdoors for much of the school year in most regions of the United States. Other Swallowtail host plants are dill and fennel. Monarch butterflies lay eggs on milkweed. Several varieties of milkweed are native to Canada, but grow throughout the United States as far south as Mexico. Painted Lady butterflies prefer thistle weed. Try these plants in sunny areas and watch the butterflies come!

Herb Garden. An herb garden provides many learning opportunities. Parsley, sage, rosemary, thyme, dill, and mint are easy-to-grow staples. Parsley will also provide a place for butterflies to lay eggs, as will dill. Students will find that herbs have distinct aromas. Try having students close their eyes and rub various herbs on their hands, then identify the herbs by their scents. Dill will remind students of pickles, and mint will remind them of gum or candy. Tell students that kitchen gardens in colonial America were planted with a variety of herbs that were used for seasoning and preserving food, for mixing medicines, for creating toiletries, and even for making housekeeping products! Have students research the roles that herbs played in early American households.

Variations for Outdoor Classroom Planning

Vegetable Garden. Vegetable gardens can be used in many ways. Here are just a few ideas: Kindergarten students studying traditions can plant vegetables as soon as school starts, and use the vegetables they harvest in their own Thanksgiving feast. Math students can use information on seed packets to determine the amount of space each plant needs to grow and how many seeds they need to fill up their garden. Students can practice measuring skills by planting seeds at the correct distances apart. Another idea is to have students plant pumpkin seeds and predict the size of the pumpkins!

Native American Garden. Students can explore Native American culture firsthand as they plant corn, squash, and beans together to create a "three sisters" garden. Native American tribes planted one seed from each plant in the same hills. This created an ecosystem with a natural fertilizing effect. It also provided a series of harvests instead of just one. Crops that complement each other are still used in practices such as crop rotation. In addition to the science used in this system of companion planting, there are many legends connected to the "three sisters" that you can employ for language arts connections. Another option for a Native American garden: plant pole beans on rods that lean in to form a teepee, under which students can sit. More idea-starters may be found at the U.S. Bureau of Indian Affairs at http://www.doi.gov/bureau-indian-affairs.html.

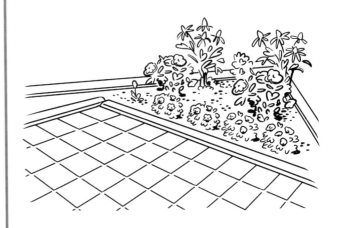

Perennial Garden. Since perennial plants regenerate year after year, a perennial garden is a good financial investment. Perennials provide great science study, but also connect with other subjects; for example, art teachers at some schools have requested perennials as subjects for drawing for their students. Perennials either come back from the same roots and stem each spring or do not completely die back during the winter. Grasses such as purple fountain grass or zebra grass are attractive additions to any outdoor classroom. A number of varieties of nandina keep their leaves throughout the school year and provide vibrant colors seasonally. Other perennials include flowers such as bleeding hearts and violets, and plants such as hostas and astilbes. Many perennials need to be divided as they mature, so if you have parents with perennials in their gardens, they can provide you with free divisions of the growing plants for your outdoor learning lab-classroom.

Outdoor Classroom Components

Many outdoor-classroom components below were originally designed for sixth graders, but can easily be adapted for elementary school students. The intended lessons would work well in upper elementary school.

Archaeological Dig. This is a sandbox where teachers can bury "artifacts" and parts of skeletons for students to retrieve and assemble. The teaching objective is to show how to use a grid to mark dig finds. Plastic skeletons are available from some science suppliers, and often in toy departments or dollar stores as well. Clay flowerpots, broken into pieces that students can reassemble and glue, are also great items for retrieval.

Compost Bins. Choose different types of compost bins to use for lunch scraps and yard waste for comparison and contrast. Before you select bins, be sure to check your local ordinances. Many cities and towns have laws describing the various kinds of compost bins that are allowed within city limits. A simple bin can be made from inexpensive hog-wire or chicken wire, stretched around four posts that are secured in the ground. Compost bins can also be purchased from garden centers and science catalogues. If you have more than one bin, students can use thermometers to compare temperatures in different bins.

Compass Rose. Use stones to make a permanent compass rose on the ground. A volunteer who is a brick mason might be willing to build a compass rose as a donation, perhaps involving your students in the process so that they could learn about and share his or her skills.

Human Sundial. Students can tell time by casting their own shadows on a series of markers on the ground. Use landscape timbers to mark each hour where a human shadow falls. You can verify placement with a watch and a compass. The person whose shadow you use should face north, and can increase the length of the shadow by holding both arms straight up above his or her head. This feature is a student favorite!

Pond. Life-science classes benefit greatly from testing water samples, observing cells in water plants, and perhaps even viewing the life cycle of a frog in their own pond. However, be aware that having a small pond requires an increased amount of maintenance. If you want a circulating pump to prevent water from becoming stagnant, you will also have the expense of electricity. A simpler and less expensive solution is to build a shallow bog that is basically a muddy, damp place. You can use the bog to establish plants.

Building a Temporary Outdoor Classroom

What can you do if your plans have been turned down, or if you do not have the space, money, time, or energy to build an outdoor classroom-learning lab? Fortunately, there are some practical, short-term alternatives. Here is how to adapt outdoor-classroom components for temporary use.

Archaeological Dig. Look for a small plastic swimming pool on sale at the end of the summer. Fill it about halfway with play sand and bury your artifacts. A miniature archaeological dig can be set up in smaller plastic containers. Adjust the size of the artifacts to suit the size of the container.

Attracting Birds and Butterflies. Feeders for birds and butterflies can hang on shepherd's hooks near your classroom window. You can also find feeders that attach to windows with suction cups. Butterflies are attracted to colorful feeders similar to hummingbird feeders. Fill these feeders with a mixture of four parts water to one part sugar. Ask parents to donate a birdhouse, which can be placed in a tree in a convenient schoolyard location.

Compost Bins. Use plastic containers to compost food scraps (from plants) indoors. If you are on a strict budget, use small leftover plastic food containers—any plastic containers that can be sealed will do—and fill them with a variety of leaves and kitchen scraps. Be prepared for the strong odor when you open them. If you open the containers outdoors, the smell will be quickly diffused. In addition, some science companies sell worm farms or habitats, which allow students to study how earthworms speedup the composting process. These products are made for indoor use.

Gardens. You may think that nothing can beat a great outdoor garden, but container gardens can come in a close second, and their portability makes them acceptable to even the most conservative administrator. To make them lightweight, fill the bottoms of deeper containers with broken pieces of foam. Use high-quality potting soil for the best results, fertilizing the soil as needed. Existing flower beds on the school grounds are another option. With administrative permission, improve the look of these flower beds with some nectar flowers to attract butterflies or some berry bushes to attract birds. This can also be a great way to start building a case for an outdoor classroom later if that's your goal.

Math Patios. Find an open area in a parking lot, bus loading area, or walkway, and have students measure a ten-foot-square area. Mark it off with chalk in square feet to create an elementary hundreds-chart patio. For middle school students who need a larger space, ask them to measure and mark a 20-foot-square area. To make a math patio on grass, put stakes in the ground at four corners and create a grid with white string or brightly colored yarn.

CD-104107 *Outdoor Science Classroom*

Does Money Grow On Schoolyard Trees?

CHAPTER 2

Resources for Your Outdoor Classroom

You may find activities in this book that really excite you, but how will you pay for them? Money does not grow on trees, even the trees in a schoolyard. The good news is that schools are nonprofit organizations eligible for thousands of dollars in grant funding each year. Schools are also the beneficiary of many charitable individuals, corporations, community leaders, and parents.

Your challenge as an environmental educator is to channel those grant funds, the donations of goods and services, and volunteer help from parents and the community into projects to help your students participate in exciting outdoor lessons.

While there is some degree of luck and chance to receiving donations and grant money, there are some tried and true ways to enhance your chances. One of the most important skills for success is persuasive writing and communication skills. If you do not think of yourself as a good writer, find a colleague whose writing skills you respect. Ask him or her to read over grant applications you have written, or to edit letters to parents or local businesses.

Another challenge that you must overcome is being discouraged when a request for donations is denied or when an application is rejected. Grant writing offers particular challenges to the teacher who wants to stay motivated and remain focused on success, because of the rejection rate. Some grant writers say the rate of acceptance is frequently one in ten, but with practice, you can increase your odds.

All these efforts may seem like too much work in your already stretched-thin schedule. How can you motivate yourself to launch into fund-raising? Make it your goal to teach outdoor lessons that are fully funded by donations or grants. Tell yourself that teaching outdoors should not stress your own wallet. It should be a stress-free joy for both you and your students.

This chapter includes letters to parents, business partners, and community leaders that you can use or adapt to your needs as you seek money for your project. The checklist on page 26—along with the tips, list of resources, and advice in this chapter—will help you get your grant-writing effort organized and on the right track. With planning and thought, you can synchronize your fund-raising to bring together exactly the resources you need for your outdoor teaching experience.

Letters to Parents, Business Partners, and Other Donors

Parents can be your greatest ally in teaching outdoors if you keep them informed and involved. They can quash your plans if they do not understand what you are attempting to do. How can parents help?

- They can loan tools and donate supplies for the outdoor classroom building phase.
- They can provide plants from their own gardens and yards.
- They can donate their time for building, maintaining, or adding to an outdoor classroom-learning lab.
- They can provide individual skills or resources from their jobs or companies.
- They can be cheerleaders for outdoor learning within the community.

Engaging parents' interest and help with your project will also help your students. Involved parents will be enthusiastic to hear news about outdoor classroom building and lessons, creating more enthusiasm among your students.

As with any letter home to parents, the letter about teaching outdoors should be both friendly and professional. It should help them to feel comfortable with the idea that their child will be learning outdoors in ways that they may not have heard of before. The letter should also make feel parents welcome to join you in some of the outdoor activities you have planned for your students.

Community leaders and business partners are also vital sources of supplies and resources. How can members of the community help?

- They can donate money to buy expensive supplies or maintenance equipment.
- They can provide special services, such as installing benches or putting in patios.
- They can provide valuable networking connections that may lead to other involvement within the community.
- They can provide publicity, such as a local newspaper article, that may attract the attention of other potential donors.

Whenever you send out a letter, think carefully about the purpose of your communication with parents or business partners. Some sample letters are included in this chapter. If they fit your situation, you can simply copy them, fill in the blanks, and send them out. Or, these letters can serve as models for more individualized letters that you write yourself. The letters included ask for donations, ask for volunteers, and announce that you are planning an outdoor classroom. Choose one that best fits your situation, or combine them as needed.

Make sure your administrator first approves what you plan to do outdoors, and that he or she approves the letters to parents or community leaders before they are sent out. It is best if your administrator is supportive and enthusiastic about you stepping out of the box, or in this case stepping out of the building.

Letter to Parents

Donations Needed for Outdoor Lesson Supplies

Date: _____

Dear Parents,

During this school year, we will be conducting a number of lessons outdoors to help our students use real-life situations as they learn about science, social studies, writing, and math. Research has shown that learning in the context of the natural environment raises student achievement. We would like to take advantage of the opportunities that await our students just outside the doors of our school.

In order to teach outdoors effectively, there are some items we need that are not in the school budget. When the cost of everything together is added up, this seems like a costly venture. But as single items, most of these things are not expensive. If every family could contribute one or two items, that would help us tremendously. The items we need are listed below.

_____   _____

_____   _____

_____   _____

_____   _____

_____   _____

If you have any questions about the items on the list or about our outdoor lessons, please feel free to call me at _____. Please remember that donations such as these are completely voluntary. Although the overall number of donations may affect how we carry out our plans, all students will be taking part in our outdoor lessons regardless of whether or not their families make donations.

Thank you for considering a contribution. I hope that you will hear from your child about how we used your donations, or that you will have the chance to see us firsthand as we work in our "outdoor classroom."

Sincerely,

Letter to Parents

Outdoor Volunteers Needed for Work Day

Date: _____

Dear Parents,

As you know, we are conducting some of our lessons outdoors this year. Research has shown that learning in the natural environment raises student achievement, and we want your child to have this advantage. In order to make this possible, we need your help.

Parents can help us by volunteering to complete the tasks listed below. Parents and students will have the opportunity to work side by side. If you have tools and work gloves that you can bring, that will be helpful.

(**Return bottom portion.**)

- -

Tasks to complete: (Check if you can help.)

_____   _____

_____   _____

_____   _____

Tools we need to borrow: (Circle those you can bring.)

_____   _____

_____   _____

Name of Parent _____   Student _____

Daytime Phone _____   Home Phone _____

If you do not have tools that we can borrow, we can still use your time and energy! Please fill out the bottom half of this letter to let us know how you can help. And feel free to call me at _____ if you have questions.

Thank you,

Letter to Parents

Building an Outdoor Classroom

Date: _____

Dear Parents,

Research has shown that student achievement is raised when the natural environment is used as a context for learning. Our school is planning an outdoor classroom where students can study in garden areas designed to fit our curriculum.

As you can imagine, an outdoor classroom can be costly, but we hope, with the involvement of our parents and the community, the project can be done without additional financial burden on the school. Some of the ways you can help are to give us your time, your services, extra plants from your yard, and/or garden tools.

If you have plants that you would like to share with us, please list them below so we can fit them into our garden plan. If you would like to be on the outdoor classroom volunteer list, please sign up to help in that capacity. If you are handy with woodwork, perhaps you can offer to build some bird houses or bird feeders for us. If you have experience or expertise in gardening or another environmental area, you could offer advice as we work on our outdoor classroom or provide us with information for our lessons.

Please show how you can help below and return the bottom portion of this letter to our classroom. Feel free to call me at _____ if you have questions. Any donation you can make to our outdoor classroom is greatly appreciated!

Sincerely,

(**Return bottom portion.**)

_____ I would like to be on a list of outdoor classroom volunteers.

_____ I can donate _____ _____ plants.
               Number   Type
_____ I can provide these services: _____

Name of Parent _____ Student _____

Daytime Phone _____ Home Phone _____

CD-104107 *Outdoor Science Classroom*

Letter to Business Partners & Community Members

Assistance Needed for Outdoor Lessons

School: _____   Phone: _____

Date: _____

Our school is taking on the task of teaching environmental lessons outdoors in the schoolyard. We plan to create an outdoor learning experience for students to enhance science, math, and language arts lessons.

This is an expensive proposition, but we know that with the help of community leaders and business partners we can accomplish it. That's why we're coming to you for support of these important educational goals.

As we have reviewed our plans for teaching outdoors, we thought that you may be able to help us with the following goods or services:

_____

_____

_____

Any donations you make to our school, a nonprofit organization, are tax-deductible. We hope that you will look favorably upon our request. If you are unable to give everything that we have asked for, perhaps you can still fulfill part of our request. We also would welcome volunteer hours from your employees. We will be contacting you personally to follow up, but please feel free to call us at _____ if you have questions.

Thank you for your support of our school. Together, schools and business partners can build a better workforce for the future.

Sincerely,

_____

Teacher

_____

Principal

CD-104107 *Outdoor Science Classroom*

Professional Growth Through Grant Writing

Does the idea of writing a grant proposal intimidate you? You're not alone. Let's be frank: grant writing can be frustrating. But it can also be rewarding—in fact, one of the most positive experiences of your career. Why? Because it can help you provide experiences for your students that you never dreamed could be financially possible. This chapter provides you with tools to help you write a successful grant. So, dream big! Think about what you and your students can accomplish with some financial backing.

The tips in this book have come from direct experience in writing grants. One of the reasons it can be frustrating is because you get no specific feedback on grant applications, successful or not. You either get a "congratulations," or a "thank you for applying." If you really want to build on your successes, keep your own records. Compare a successful application to one that was not successful. What could you have changed to make the unsuccessful grant better?

Each time you apply for a grant, read two or three old applications that you have kept on file. That will jog your memory about the appeals and details that work, and those that do not work. Some organizations that provide grant funding will give you summaries of successful grants upon written request. Others provide a synopsis on a Web site. Take advantage of this opportunity and study the examples to see what you can do to polish your request and make your own application stronger.

If you can juggle the responsibilities of teaching school successfully, you can write a grant that gets funded. It may not happen the first time, but it will happen if you are persistent. As teachers we constantly insist that students not give up, but we are apt to do so ourselves. Remember, somebody has to be the one person in ten that gets her grant funded. Decide today that you will be that person. Make it happen!

Grant Writing Tips and Strategies

Before you begin searching for grant resources and writing applications, ask yourself some key questions and jot down your answers.

- What project am I planning to do?
- How am I planning to do the project?
- What materials do I need and how much will they cost?

If you have answers for these three questions, then you have the backbone of a decent grant application. The goal is to take it from decent to dazzling so that those who read the application have no choice but to fund your request! Follow the "Top Ten Tips" on pages 24 and 25 and use the checklist on page 26 to help you accomplish this.

One of the most important ways you can gain the confidence you need to write grants is to think about plans for your students that could require grant funding. Teachers who consistently plan "extra" activities for their students generally have what it takes to carry out those plans. That enthusiasm is what will gain you the grant money you need, as long as your enthusiasm, knowledge, and need show on your application. Remember that the average acceptance of grant applications is only one in ten, so increase your odds by making the application excellent. And think about applying for more than one grant at a time. The worst that can happen is that the answer is "no." Good luck!

Top Ten Tips for Grant Writing

"Not failure, but low aim, is sin."
— Dr. Benjamin E. Mays

The following tips have been based on years of successful grant writing, and present a game plan that has consistently brought positive results.

Have a good plan.

Whatever you would like to do with the grant money you receive, make sure you have a well-planned project that either addresses a need at your school, or enriches your students' experience. The plan should address the "big picture" and cover all aspects of accomplishing your goal.

Match the need to the grant.

Whatever grant you apply for, make certain that it is intended for the type of project you have in mind. Some grants are more general than others, but most have guidelines that will let you know if your idea fits the grant's intentions. Be sure to do your homework; it will save time and rejections.

Read the application carefully.

Read the application two or three times before writing the first word of the grant. Familiarize yourself with the application by taking notes on separate paper as you read it. What part of your idea goes where on the application? What words on the application give you clues about which features of your project to highlight most prominently?

Get the approval of your administrator.

Before you spend every night for a week working on a lengthy grant application, make sure you share your idea with your principal. (Make a point of sharing the completed grant application later, too.) Most applications will require your principal's signature or a letter of recommendation.

Get started, and get started early.

Even if you have never written a successful grant before, write *something* on the paper to get it started. Your train of thought cannot develop if you don't get it in motion. One completed paragraph will encourage and excite you more than you think. Also, start on the grant application long before the deadline. It will take longer than you think, and the signatures and approvals after you finish writing will add time to the completion process.

Get personal advice from successful grant writers.

If you know any teachers who have received a grant, talk to them about it. Attend a grant-writing session at a professional meeting. There is no substitute for the one-on-one advice and exchange of ideas between the experienced and novice grant writers.

Top Ten Tips for Grant Writing

Find a trustworthy colleague to offer proofreading and advice.

No matter how good a writer you are, you will need a great proofreader. You might need to go to a colleague that is an acquaintance rather than a friend to make sure you are getting true feedback from someone who doesn't mind "hurting your feelings." Choose a person who has excellent communication skills. You require honest, professional, constructive criticism to help make your application as strong as it can be. Once you get advice and suggested changes, be sure to make use of the proofreader when completing your finished draft.

Find a grant-writing buddy.

In addition to a proofreader, an experiences advisor, and a supportive administrator, look for a colleague who is at your level and buddy up with that person. Use e-mail, the telephone, or face-to-face meetings to support each other through the grant-writing and application process. If you find a buddy from another school, you'll be able to share information without competing against one another. Many grants are awarded to only one applicant per school during a school year, or sometimes you can only win once. If you and your buddy both have successful grants, trade copies of your applications. Then each of you can apply for the grant the other received during the following year.

Apply for two grants simultaneously.

You may not want to do this your first time around, but after you have had some success and experience at grant writing, choose a project you want funded and apply for two grants at one time. You'll have a better chance of getting the project funded, and you can follow your checklist and steps for both applications at the same time. Make sure to keep your papers separate, and you can double your chances.

Believe in yourself.

No matter how good a teacher you are, the grant-writing application can be hard on your ego and on your confidence level. Don't let it get to you. Many teachers who successfully win grants have talent, but they also have unbridled self-confidence, and that belief in themselves pulls them through the inevitable rejections on the road to their final successes. Focus on your goals and believe that you have the staying power to see them through. If you do that, you've won half the battle.

Grant-Writing Checklist

Write dates or notes in the blanks to keep track of your process.

Task	Started	Completed	Need Signature	Other
Preliminary tasks				
Plan mapped out				
Grant matches need				
Carefully read application				
Administrative approval of project				
Deadline is reasonable				
Proofreader/advisor agrees to help				
Getting it done				
Budget plan outlined				
Writing starts				
Matching funds secured				
Shopped for itemized budget				
Necessary signatures obtained				
Final version printed and copied				
Envelope prepared and mailed on time				
Follow up				
Results received				
Records filed				
Receipts kept				
Publicity, if successful				
More tasks				

CD-104107 *Outdoor Science Classroom*

"It is not a disgrace not to reach the stars,
but it is a disgrace to have no stars to reach for."
– Dr. Benjamin E. Mays

Grant money is available for nearly any project you plan for your school. Search the Internet; materials from professional organizations; information from professional seminars/conferences; educational journals; colleges/universities; and even some of the junk mail that you receive at school. The following list is by no means exhaustive, but nevertheless a good place to start for grants related to teaching outdoors. Many applications can be downloaded, and some can be filled out on-line.

State and Local Resources

In every state and in many local school systems, there are grant resources available only to teachers in that state or county. Look for links to state science organizations at the NSTA (National Science Teachers Association) Web site. Many of these groups offer state grants and teacher awards with cash prizes. For local resources, find the person in the school system who is a grants contact or coordinator. This person can usually give you some ideas for resources. You might also contact your local United Way or county extension service to find out if these organizations offer grant funding.

Grants for Science, Math, and Gardening

www.kidsgardening.com
National Youth Garden Grants
Greenhouse Grants
Dutch Bulb Grants
Healthy Sprouts Award
($250 to $2,495 in garden products or cash grants)

www.nsta.org
National Science Teachers Association Teacher Awards & Competitions ($1,000 to $1,500 in cash grants directly to teachers)
Toyota Tapestry Awards ($2,500 to $10,000)
Shell Science Teaching Award ($10,000)

www.nwf.org
National Wildlife Federation ($3,000 to $7,000)
Grants to nonprofits for "on-the-ground" efforts to save endangered species
Note: Partner with a non-profit for this program.

www.nsf.gov
National Science Foundation
Presidential Awards for Excellence in Science & Mathematics Teaching ($10,000)
Note: Cash awards to teachers who have demonstrated exceptional performance

www.toshiba.com/taf/
Toshiba American Foundation (Grants in varying amounts, averaging $5,000)

www.nctm.org
National Council of Teachers of Mathematics
Mathematics Education Trust (MET) ($2,000 grants for classroom projects or continuing education)
Toyota TIME grants ($10,000)

General Grant Information
www.schoolfundingresources.org
www.schoolgrants.org
www.grantsalert.com
www.schoolfundingservices.org
www.ed.gov/free

Outdoor classes give teachers the chance to share nature's wonders with students, firsthand. From the smallest insect to the largest flying predator, children will retain far more knowledge from watching animals in natural settings than from simply reading about them.

One of the most important concepts to share with students is that animals have four basic needs: sources for food, a water source, shelter, and space to bring up their young. In planning an outdoor learning experience, think about how many of these resources are already available on the school grounds, and what you can add to make the environment more hospitable for wildlife.

Among the wild animals that may travel through a schoolyard, birds, bugs, and butterflies are the most universal—the focus of most of the lessons in this chapter. There is an abundance of information for teaching about these animals that is available through the Internet, books, and nature centers.

As you develop your outdoor-teaching skills, you may want to bring a wider variety of wildlife into your lessons. You must take into consideration the safety of your students and the location of your school when thinking about attracting wildlife. Animals that move through the air are less of a nuisance and therefore more acceptable in the schoolyard and the surrounding area, regardless if the school is located in an urban or rural setting.

For many birds, shelter could be as simple as trees that are already living in your schoolyard. Water might be available in a stream or ditch, or you could easily set up a birdbath. Depending on the species, a food source might be insects living naturally in the area, seeds from flowering plants, or several bird feeders that can be viewed from your classroom window.

Butterflies need flowers for their food sources as adults, and host plants as a food source for their caterpillars (and a place to raise their young). They also need shallow pans of sand and water for "puddling," and shrubs, fence posts, or trees on which they may climb to form their chrysalides.

Finally, space or a place to raise young must not be overlooked. The more space you have, the more area that is available for animals to establish their own territories, which is particularly important for students to compare the habits of various species. You can increase the appeal of the schoolyard to certain birds by adding birdhouses. Many students will enjoy building and placing the houses as well.

The following activities may lead to establishing permanent additions to your schoolyard or having your schoolyard certified by the National Wildlife Federation as a National Schoolyard Wildlife Habitat (**www.nwf.org**). Even if they don't, however, sharing these close-up views of animal environments will teach students valuable lessons in being good citizens in the natural world and make science concepts more meaningful, fun, and easy to recall.

CD-104107 *Outdoor Science Classroom*

Teaching with This Chapter

This chapter offers a variety of activities to help you "tame" the wildlife into helping you teach! Instructions for each lesson are presented first to help you make the most of each handout. Handouts for the activities start on page 37.

Animal Habitat Survey

Teaching Objective: To identify the basic needs of food, water, shelter, and space required by animals to raise their young; to identify resources to meet the basic needs of animals living on the school grounds

Materials: handout, clipboard, pencil

Procedures and Tips: For this lesson, it would be helpful for you to take a walk through the schoolyard before taking your students out. Look for specific examples that meet the needs of animals. Make notes about possible animal habitats.

Before leading the class outdoors, engage students in a discussion of the basic needs of animals. Animals need food, water, shelter, and space to raise young. Discuss these needs and relate them to the resources on the school grounds.

First, talk about what animals eat and drink. Some examples to mention might be that squirrels eat nuts and seeds from trees; spiders eat insects; and caterpillars eat leaves. Water sources for animals can include mud puddles; water dripping from a gutter on the building; streams; or birdbaths.

Shelter for animals can be trees, the eaves of the school building, and rocks or underbrush. Space for raising young connects to shelter, and can include trees for some animals and open fields for others.

After students have had a chance to explore outdoors and identify a number of these ideas, gather them back into a group to discuss the results of their schoolyard survey. If you are still planning your outdoor classroom, this activity can allow students to help adjust and improve the plans. What have they found that meets animals' basic needs, and what can they identify that is lacking?

Birds: An Example of Animal Adaptation

Teaching Objective: To identify examples of animal adaptations in birds

Materials: handout, clipboard, pencil, binoculars (optional for bird watching)

Procedures and Tips: Discuss animal adaptations in the classroom before you go outdoors. You may wish to read out loud from a resource book or watch a video about animal adaptations to offer students background information.

When going outdoors to observe birds, remind students to be quiet and still. Birds will frequently be scared away by noise and movement. One way to view birds with an active class is to sit far away from the spot where birds gather. You will need binoculars for conducting the activity this way. If you don't have bird feeders, preview the schoolyard for trees where birds live. You may be able to spot nests ahead of time and find the best place on the school grounds to take your students.

If you have little luck with natural attraction of birds to the school grounds, try scattering mixed birdseed in a field or along the edge of a wooded area. If you see that this works, make it part of the observation by letting your students in on the strategy. Compare what happens when the seed is scattered to when it is not.

The Great American Backyard Bird Count

Teaching Objectives: To engage students in a wildlife counting activity; to connect students with the scientific community

Materials: handout, clipboard, pencil, binoculars, Internet access to **www.birds.cornell.edu**

Procedures and Tips: Counting birds and other animals is an activity that scientists have conducted throughout modern times, and one that is easy and engaging for your students. This is another activity that will benefit from your scoping out the bird populations in your schoolyard ahead of time. A preview will give you an idea of some reasonable numbers to expect from your students when they do their count.

If possible, place a number of bird feeders on your school grounds to increase your chances of seeing a variety of birds. Consider offering sunflowers seeds in one feeder, thistle seed in another, and mixed seed in a third feeder. You may even spread seed on the ground if feeders are not within your budget. Actually, there are certain kinds of songbirds that are ground feeders.

You can make a temporary bird feeder by rolling a pine cone first in peanut butter and then in birdseed. Tie it to a tree branch with string.

After your students have conducted their observations and compared them in small groups, facilitate a class discussion about their discoveries. Ask students if the results might be different in another season. (Migration would affect fall and spring numbers in many areas.) If you plan to conduct the activity again, save the handouts and compare the results the next time. This will yield a nice opportunity to graph results if students observe differences.

If your school has a computer lab, have your class visit the Internet site for Cornell's ornithology lab (see materials list). Even if you do not have Internet access for your students, visit the Cornell University Web site yourself before you teach this lesson for additional background information.

Do You Hear What I Hear?

Teaching Objectives: To identify the role of animal sounds in nature; to compare and contrast the sounds made by various animals

Materials: CD or tape of nature sounds, CD player or stereo, handout, clipboard, timer or watch with a second hand

Procedures and Tips: Shop around for CDs or tapes of animal sounds that you can play for your class. Some of these recordings have themes such as "rain forest" or "ocean." Listen to the recording ahead of time and choose the part that has the largest number of distinct animal sounds. If possible, use a recording that has sounds native to your area.

To set the mood when you play the sounds for the class, turn the lights low and/or have students close their eyes. Ask students to listen for at least two minutes (more if possible). Ask them to write down as many different animals as they can identify. Ask them to be specific about animals (e.g., don't specify birds, but owls, seagulls, hawks, etc.).

As in other lessons, preview the schoolyard to determine if there are sounds that are audible and plentiful. (If not, try listening outdoors at home at night and consider making this a homework assignment.) After students have listened to recorded and real animal sounds, have them discuss why animals make sounds. Research the topic with books from your media center or on the Internet. If you or your students have tape recorders, you can try recording nature sounds at night to share with the class. There are numerous extensions for this activity, such as comparing the sounds of nature in different biomes, at different times of day, or in various places in your community.

The Migration Sensation

Teaching Objective: To identify animals that migrate through the local area; to provide an understanding of the advantages of migration

Materials: handout, pencil, clipboard, resources for research, paper for brochure, bird feeders for migrating birds (optional), flowers for migrating butterflies (optional), digital camera for brochure pictures (optional)

Procedures and Tips: If your students have completed the activity "Birds: An Example of Animal Adaptations," then they will have a head start on this

lesson. That is because migration can be taught from the perspective of being the ultimate adaptation. In other words, migrating animals adapt to a totally new environment when the current one becomes difficult. After discussing this concept with the class, take a walk through your schoolyard or outdoor classroom. Have your students take their handout on a clipboard to answer questions 1 and 3. Question 2 can be done after you go back inside. As you are walking through the schoolyard, tell students to think about how they might make a travel brochure for migrating animals. If you have access to a digital camera, students may take pictures to use in their brochures.

Discuss the answers in cooperative groups or as a whole class. Then have students work on their brochures. Some computer software programs have templates for brochures, which may help students with design ideas.

Migration Mapping

Teaching Objectives: To identify migration routes of animals; to compare and contrast the migration routes of two animals

Materials: handout, ruler, blue and red markers, research materials (books or Internet access to **www.learner.org/jnorth**)

Procedures and Tips: Have students observe in the schoolyard and then research migration routes on the Journey North Internet site or in other sources. Ask them to use the map on the handout to trace the migration routes of any two animals that migrate through your area. If there are numerous animals with migration routes through your area, you may wish to divide the students into groups and assign two animals to each group. After they complete the activity, students can post their maps in the room, or put their lines of migration onto a group map. For the group map, use a copy machine to enlarge the map on the reproducible, and use additional colors to make it easier to see different routes.

Monarch Butterfly Life Cycle

Teaching Objectives: To identify by sight the stages of the monarch butterfly and its host plant

Materials: handout, crayons, colored pencils or water-based markers, Internet access to **www.monarchwatch.org**

Procedures and Tips: This activity would be a good first lesson whether you decide to raise monarch caterpillars in your classroom or to search for the adult butterflies and their offspring on milkweed plants. There are about two dozen species of milkweed including common milkweed, tropical, swamp, sand vine, and narrow leaf. A complete guide to milkweed including photographs and information about various species can be found on the Monarch Watch Web site at **www.monarchwatch.org/milkweed/guide/index.htm**.

More than just a coloring exercise, the point of the handout is to show the monarch and the host plant as it appears in nature. Use the multimedia gallery on **www.monarchwatch.org** to make sure all of the stages depicted on the handout are colored correctly. There are various shades of orange in the monarch wings, and it may be a good time to mix in a lesson about creating different shades of paint colors.

Provide students with crayons, water-based markers, and colored pencils instead of limiting them to one medium.

Discuss with the students that the adult butterfly drinks the nectar from the flowers and lays eggs on the underside of the milkweed leaves—only one egg per plant. The caterpillar eats the leaves. Emphasize that milkweed plants provides food, shelter, and a place to raise monarch young.

Tag, You're It!

Teaching Objectives: To practice methods used by scientists in tracking migration of monarch butterflies; to participate in genuine scientific research as a part of the international scientific community

Materials: monarch butterflies (raised from caterpillars or captured wild), tags from Monarch Watch, butterfly nets, containers for butterflies, handout, clipboard, Internet access to **www.monarchwatch.org**

Procedures and Tips: Before teaching this lesson, visit the Monarch Watch Web site well in advance to order tags. If you do not have Internet access, you can call Monarch Watch at 1-888-TAGGING for information on ordering tags. This is a fall activity, so plan on conducting this lesson between August and October. Once you receive the tags, you may wish to practice tagging a live butterfly on your own before you do so with your class. You may also wish to consider doing this as a demonstration lesson. Students should thoroughly research the Monarch Watch Web site before attempting this activity.

In addition to the instructions on-line, you will also receive tagging instructions with your tags. The main thing to emphasize with students is to be gentle with the butterflies. If you are capturing the butterflies wild, they tend to be far more active than if you raise them from caterpillars. Therefore, you may want to consider raising caterpillars if this is your first time working with monarchs. (Note to those schools located west of the Rocky Mountains: Contact the Oregon Department of Agriculture, 635 Capitol St. NE, Salem, OR 97310, for information on tagging the western population of monarchs. Monarch Watch only tags monarchs located east of the Rockies.)

Paper "Migration" of Monarch Butterflies

Teaching Objectives: To link cultural and geographical impacts of migration to science content; to practice map skills

Materials: handout, crayons or markers, large mailing envelope and postage, Internet access to **www.learner.org/jnorth**

Procedures and Tips: This project usually has a mid-October deadline, so plan ahead by visiting the Journey North Web site during the summer or at the very start of the school year to locate all of the information on this paper butterfly exchange between American and Mexican students.

In creating their paper butterflies for the "migration," your students may use the pattern provided on the reproducible to make their paper butterflies, or create their own monarch butterfly design. The finished

work must be flat and not multi-dimensional. Students should include a friendly message to Mexican students, in which they might encourage their new friends to preserve the habitats of the monarch butterfly and other wildlife.

When all of your students have colored their butterflies and written their messages, gather the butterflies and mail them in a large envelope to Journey North. Make sure to include a self-addressed, stamped envelope of about the same size as your mailing envelope. This will carry Mexican butterflies from the Journey North offices back to your school in the spring. Journey North orchestrates this activity for teachers. The "migration" is supported by the Internet site with updates on the location of the paper butterflies, making comparisons to the route and progress of the real butterflies. In the spring, your class will receive paper butterflies from Mexico and perhaps other places in the United States or Canada. This will allow your students to create some interesting maps that show where the butterflies originated and the route they took to get to your school.

What Do Baby Swallowtails Swallow?

Teaching Objectives: To identify host plants of caterpillars; to make observations and inferences of the preferences of caterpillars for certain plants

Materials: fennel, dill, and parsley plants; swallowtail caterpillars; handout; clipboard; pencil

Teaching with This Chapter

Procedures and Tips: Swallowtail butterflies are one of the most common in North America. There are many varieties. Most prefer one of three herbs as host plants: fennel, dill, or parsley. With these plants, you can test the preferences of swallowtails in your area. It may even help you determine the variety of swallowtail that is native to your state.

Have students complete the following steps:

- Germinate seeds to establish plants in the garden area or purchase plants.

- Put plants in a sunny area along with some flowers for the adult butterflies. (To do this activity indoors, purchase swallowtail chrysalides from your favorite science vendor and put the mature plants inside an insect cage.)

- Observe the area until swallowtails are spotted. If none are seen, check the leaves of the plants for small white specks, which are the butterfly eggs.

- When the eggs hatch, keep a record of which plant is eaten. If more than one plant type displays eggs, compare the amount and the rate at which caterpillars eat the leaves of each plant after they hatch.

- Use the chart on page 46 to record the results. Analyze the data on the chart to determine what the swallowtails in your area prefer.

If your experiment is not successful (no butterflies were attracted and no eggs laid), research additional species of butterflies native to your area. Check a butterfly field guide, or use the Internet such as **www. butterflywebsite.com** for ideas.

What Do Adult Swallowtails Swallow?

Teaching Objectives: To make observations and inferences about animal feeding habits using butterflies as an example; to identify feeding preferences of certain butterflies

Materials: Three varieties of flowering plants, butterflies, handout, clipboard, pencil

Procedures and Tips: Use a container, a schoolyard flower garden, or a space in an outdoor classroom to plant three or more types of flowers. Then have your students observe the flowers to record which ones are most frequently visited by butterflies.

Prepare students for this activity by watching a video of a butterfly using its proboscis (feeding tube) to drink from a flower. Students will then know what to look for while making their observations in the garden.

This activity will work best if done over a period of time, with students gathering information at various times over several days or weeks. Weather and luck will play a part in this activity, so you will have to be flexible enough to make time for observations on sunny days when butterflies are active in the schoolyard. If you would rather teach this lesson indoors, a butterfly habitat with three types of flowers inside will serve the same purpose, and perhaps offer simpler observation and more predictable results.

Milk a Weed for All It's Worth!

Teaching Objectives: To identify various varieties of host plants for monarch butterflies; to gather and graph quantifiable data from observations in an experiment

Materials: Three varieties of milkweed seeds/plants, Monarch butterflies or caterpillars, flower pots, potting soil, water, trowel, handout, pencil

Procedures and Tips: Order three varieties of milkweed seed from Monarch Watch at **www. monarchwatch.org**. Germinate the seed indoors and transplant the plants outdoors when they are about 20 cm tall. Have students create a chart to gather data. Make sure the data is *quantifiable*, able to be translated into numbers for comparison. As a control in this experiment, students may choose one variety of milkweed and keep it indoors in a cage with a butterfly raised from larva to adult. You may wish to conduct the entire experiment indoors by placing pots of all three milkweed types in the insect cage with monarch butterflies.

Raising My Caterpillar

Teaching Objectives: To practice making predictions based on evidence; to observe the life cycle of a butterfly; to care for a living thing

Materials: caterpillars, small plastic container, insect cage, food source (the correct host plant leaves) for caterpillars, paper towel, stick, ruler, handout, pencil

Procedures and Tips: The easiest way to get started with caterpillars in the classroom is to order a butterfly life cycle kit from a reputable science supply company. One of the most common butterflies sold as larvae is the painted lady. These caterpillars are hearty and easy to care for. They come with their food medium, the containers, and all the directions you need. However, if you find some caterpillars which you can reliably identify by species and correct food source, you can raise them on your own without a kit. Be sure to provide students with small containers. A small plastic peanut butter jar is just about the right size. Punch holes in the top and cut a piece of paper towel to put between the lid and the lip of the jar so the caterpillar won't hurt itself trying to get out of the holes. The paper towel also makes a convenient place for the caterpillar to make its chrysalis.

Have students clean the waste out of the bottom of the jars each day, and replace any uneaten food with fresh leaves. Each student should observe his caterpillar carefully each day and record the size of the caterpillar. Keeping a science journal to describe the changes is an important step. Students can measure caterpillars through the sides of the jars most easily when the caterpillars walk up the inside of the jars.

When each caterpillar makes its chrysalis on the paper, take the paper out and wrap it around a stick. Place the stick in an insect cage. When the butterfly emerges, usually a week or so later, observe it for one day and then release it outdoors.

Note: Make sure when ordering butterfly larvae from a science supplier that the species is native to your area. After all the butterflies are released, have students compile their data and represent it on graphs.

Teaching with This Chapter

Animals Living on the School Grounds

Teaching Objectives: To compare and contrast animal adaptations in the local environment

Materials: handout, clipboard, pencil, digital camera for photographs of animals in schoolyard (optional), binoculars (optional)

Procedures and Tips: This is a culminating activity to those earlier in this chapter. Conduct at least three or four of the other schoolyard activities first (such as Animal Habitat Survey, Birds: An Example of Migration, Backyard Bird Count, Do You Hear What I Hear?). Use data from other activities: charts, handouts, graphs, or any other data from a science journal or notebook. Then have students compile the information into the chart from the reproducible.

Even though the handout uses the word "best," discuss with your students that there really is not actually a "best" animal. What they are looking for is an animal which moves with ease through the schoolyard, finds food with no trouble, and faces few predators. That animal may be the one that made the most successful adaptations in order to survive in your local area.

After compiling their individual chart information, students can work together in groups—with others who picked the same animal—to create presentations for the class. Encourage the use of computer slide shows, posters, or even role-playing as students attempt to persuade others in the class that their animal is best adapted for life in your schoolyard.

Schoolyard Food Chain

Teaching Objectives: To identify a food chain in the local environment

Materials: handout, clipboard, pencil, binoculars (optional) and hand lenses (optional)

Procedures and Tips: If you have conducted several activities in this chapter, the food chain chart information can be taken from other information gathered by your students. It is also a good culminating exercise for any unit on animals.

For their outdoor observation prior to filling out the food chain chart, students may use binoculars to get a good look at animals in trees, or use a hand lens to look under rocks and in crevices at smaller creatures. If they can't find animals, they should find evidence of their existence. Stress that in order to use animals in the chart, students need to see at least one of the animals in the chain, or at least see evidence of its existence. Some examples of a schoolyard food chain might be as follows:

1. parsley, caterpillar, spider, bird

2. wild onions, crickets, lizard, box turtle

Many other examples are sure to be discovered by your students. Check to make sure that student choices are conceivable for the environment on your school grounds.

Extension: On large sheets of drawing paper, have groups of students complete food webs using their schoolyard food chains.

Animal Habitat Survey

Directions: Take a walk on the school grounds with your teacher. Complete this form to show what resources are available to animals.

1. What sights and sounds do you see or hear that tell you animals are here?

   _____

   _____

   _____

2. What proof can you find that animals have been here? (Ex: footprints, anthills, droppings, feathers, etc.)

   _____

   _____

   _____

3. What animals may have lived here before there was a school building? What was taken away from the environment that may have made them leave?

   _____

   _____

   _____

4. Compare your findings with a partner and talk about the basic needs of the animals you wish to attract. Then check your findings with those of the rest of the class before filling in the chart below.

Basic Need of Animals	Resources in Our Schoolyard

CD-104107 *Outdoor Science Classroom*

Birds: An Example of Animal Adaptation

Directions: An *adaptation* is an adjustment, trait, or change. Animals have to make adaptations in order to survive some new change in the environment. Birds often have to adapt to changes such as new buildings, the chopping-down of trees, or less food in the area. Think about how birds have adapted to live in your area. Watch the birds that live on the school grounds and then fill in the blanks below.

1. Write down three adaptations that these birds have made to survive.

   a. _____   **b.** _____   **c.** _____

2. Compare your list with a partner. Add another adaptation from his or her list. If your lists are the same, brainstorm one more adaptation. _____

3. Next, think about the four basic needs of animals. Complete the chart below to show the needs of birds and their adaptations to their surroundings. A few examples are provided.

Basic Need	Source that Meets Need	Adaptation When Need Is Not Met
Food	(example: hunts for seeds in fields or woods)	(example: new houses are built in woods; gets seeds from birdfeeders)
Water		
Shelter	(example: builds nests in trees)	(example: trees are cut down; lives in birdhouse)
Space		

Think About It: Is migration an adaptation? Why or why not? Explain your answer on the back of this page.

Name: _____   Date: _____

The Great American Backyard Bird Count

Scientists at universities all over the world study animals. Some of the scientists at Cornell University study *ornithology*, the science of birds. See **www.birds.cornell.edu** to find out more. You can participate in the bird-counting programs that this site offers or conduct a count of your own.

Directions: Take a trip out-of-doors or watch birds from inside the classroom. Look for all different kinds of birds. Then answer the questions below.

Tip: It is helpful to sit near bird feeders for this activity. Check to see if the feeders are filled with various kinds of seeds. If you don't have bird feeders on your school grounds, try sitting near some trees. Be still and quiet so that you don't scare the birds.

1. In a 10-minute time period, how many birds did you see? _____ birds

2. How many different species of birds did you see? (You don't have to know the names to answer this

question. Just observe that they are different types.) _____

3. Which bird species did you see the most often? (If you don't know the name, describe it now and check in

a field guide later.) _____

How many of this species did you see?_____

3. Form groups of three students and compare your answers.

Who saw the greatest number of birds? _____

How many? _____

4. Would adding your numbers together be an effective way to get the total number of birds in the schoolyard?

Why or why not? _____

_____

CD-104107 *Outdoor Science Classroom*

Do You Hear What I Hear?

Evidence of animals in the wild comes in many forms. Have you ever thought of sounds as evidence? Even though you cannot hold the sounds in your hands, you can record them electronically. You can also keep a written record of what you hear.

Go outdoors with a partner. One of you will close your eyes while the other one takes notes. The student who has his eyes closed will listen first for bird sounds and then for frog sounds. The writing partner will write what sounds the partner hears. Work together for 15 minutes, taking turns. Fill in the chart below. Be sure to talk quietly, so you don't scare your test subjects!

Directions: Use a clock, timer, or stopwatch to time yourself. Every time you hear a bird or frog sound, tell your partner. The partner who is writing should make a mark in the correct column below. If you don't have birds or frogs on your school grounds, your teacher may let you choose other animal sounds to observe.

Time Interval	Bird Count	Frog Count	Other Animal	Total Sounds

Reflect: Think about the different sounds you heard on the recording your teacher played for you. Think about the sounds you heard when you listened outside. Think about other the animals you have heard, too. Why do animals make sounds? Do they respond to one another? Imagine animal sounds from another biome, such as the rain forest or the ocean. What would they sound like? Write a paragraph to answer these questions on the back of this page.

Internet Connection: Find animal sounds on the Internet. For frog sounds, search for the species "spring peepers." See if you can find the sounds of at least three different animals to share with your class.

Name: _____   Date: _____

The Migration Sensation

Is migration is the ultimate adaptation? *Migration* is the seasonal movement of animals to a completely different location. They migrate in order to survive and to meet their basic needs. Among the animals that migrate are salmon, whales, monarch butterflies, and many different kinds of birds.

Directions: Answer the questions.

Migration Through the School Grounds

1. Find out what animals migrate through your area. Spend 10 to 15 minutes making observations. Write down what you see and hear. What animals do you think might migrate through your schoolyard? What makes you think so? (Hint: Look for evidence! Do you see some birds only at certain times of the year? Do you see animals gathering to migrate? Are there animals in your schoolyard that might not want to spend the winter in your area?)

_____

_____

2. Back up your theory above with facts. Research *migration* in your media center. Look up the Journey North Web site **www.learner.org/jnorth** on the Internet. Check to see if you were right. What are some animals that actually migrate through your area?

_____

_____

3. How do the school grounds meet the needs of migrating animals? What can you and your classmates do to make the area a better place for migrating animals?

_____

_____

Show What You Know: Pretend you are a travel agent. Make a brochure that shows your schoolyard as a travel destination for migrating animals. What can you offer these animals? Read the travel section of a newspaper, a travel site on the Internet, or brochures from a local travel agent for ideas and phrases. Use these to talk about your schoolyard's best travel features. Be creative! Attract nature's "tourists" to your school!

CD-104107 *Outdoor Science Classroom*

Migration Mapping

Directions: Identify two types of animals that migrate through your state. Use the map below to trace the migration routes of these animals. Highlight the location of where you live in yellow. Put an asterisk to show the location of your town or city. Make dashes in red for one migrating animal. Make dashes in blue for the other animal. Illustrate your map with small pictures of your animals along their routes. How long does it take each animal to complete the one-way journey? If they left your school at noon today, where would they be at noon tomorrow?

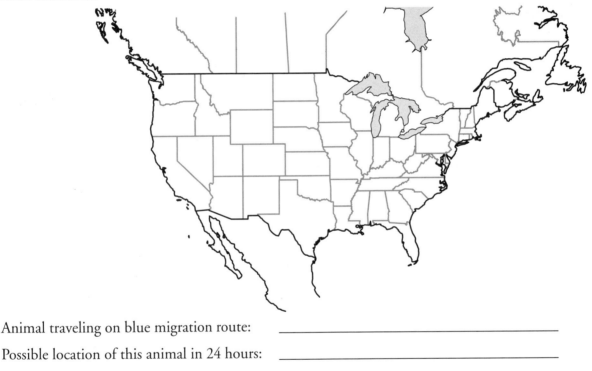

Animal traveling on blue migration route: _____

Possible location of this animal in 24 hours: _____

Animal traveling on red migration route: _____

Possible location of this animal in 24 hours: _____

Think About It: The Migrating Monarch Butterfly

Every year, millions of monarch butterflies travel from the United States and Canada to the mountains of Central Mexico. Would you like to take part in this amazing trip? Plant some milkweed seeds in your schoolyard! The butterflies find everything they need from this one plant.

It takes several generations of butterflies to travel the 2,000 miles to Mexico. Find out more about this migration on the monarch Web site **www.monarchwatch.org**. Then trace the migration routes of these insects on the map above.

CD-104107 *Outdoor Science Classroom*

Name: _____   Date: _____

Monarch Butterfly Life Cycle

Directions: Fill in the blanks to label the stages
of a monarch's life.

Word Bank

adult butterfly
caterpillar
chrysalis
egg
hanging "J"
milkweed plant

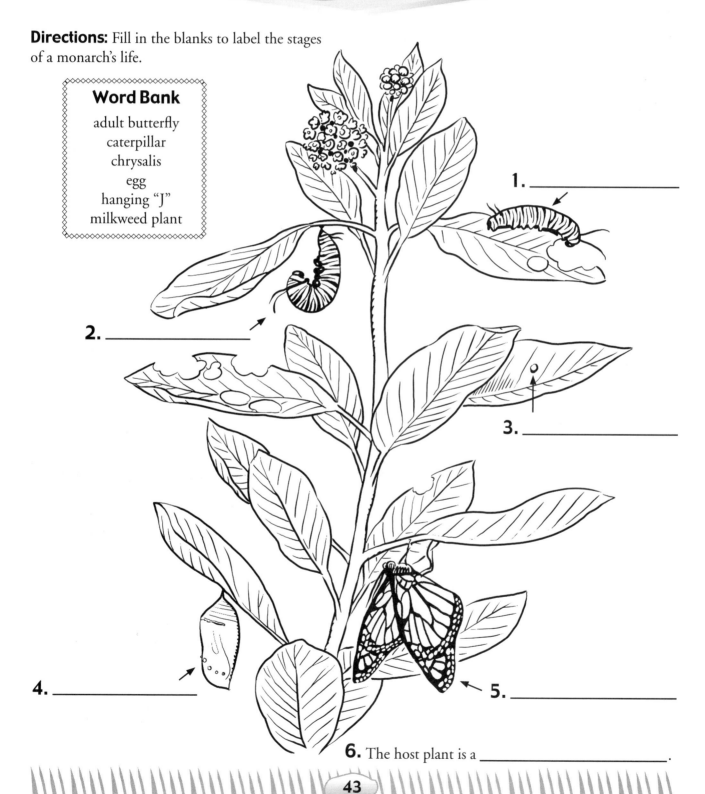

1. _____

2. _____

3. _____

4. _____

5. _____

6. The host plant is a _____.

          CD-104107 *Outdoor Science Classroom*

Name: _____   Date: _____

Tag, You're It!

You may have heard of scientists tagging birds or other animals. But have you ever heard of tagging an insect? The tagging of monarch butterflies takes place every year, and you can help. You can raise monarchs from caterpillars that your teacher provides. Or, you can locate milkweed plants and catch with a net the monarch butterflies that come to feed there. For complete tagging instructions, look on the Monarch Watch Web site **www.monarchwatch.org** and study the pictures.

Directions: Think about the questions as you tag your butterfly. Record your answers below.

1. Why would scientists want to tag butterflies? _____

_____

2. What problems might there be in designing a tag for such a small animal?

_____

_____

3. How is the information used from a tagged butterfly? _____

_____

4. How can we help the monarchs along their journey? _____

_____

5. How can the governments of Canada, the United States, and Mexico work together to help the migration of the monarch butterfly? _____

_____

Helpful Hints

Tagging a monarch butterfly is tricky to say the least! In order to tag it, you have to touch the butterfly's wings. This has to be done carefully so that the butterfly is not hurt. The trick is to hold the butterfly from the underside. This will keep the scales on the wings from rubbing off on your fingers. Be gentle. Make sure the tag is in the middle of the lower wing. The tag will not hurt the butterfly. It will not keep it from flying.

Show What You Know

Use this activity to spark your imagination! Write a newspaper article announcing the coming of monarchs to your community. Your teacher can even help you send your article to the editor of your local newspaper.

        CD-104107 *Outdoor Science Classroom*

Paper "Migration" of Monarch Butterflies

Each year, students across America and Mexico send paper butterflies to each other. This "migration" is in honor of the real monarch butterfly migration.

Directions:

1. Color or paint the butterfly on this page. Show correct monarch colors.
2. Write a message to the Mexican student who will get your butterfly. Ask the student to help protect the monarch butterflies and their habitat.
3. Look at the Journey North Internet site **www.learner.org/jnorth**. Follow the directions to send in your paper butterflies. If you live in the United States or Canada, you will do this step in the fall.
4. Paper butterflies will "migrate" back to your school in the spring. They will be sent from students in Mexico. The paper butterflies will arrive at the same time the real butterflies start to fly north!

CD-104107 *Outdoor Science Classroom*

What Do Butterflies Eat?

Read the information about butterflies.

> Butterflies have one of nature's unique adaptations: *metamorphosis*. This means they completely change in form at different stages of their lives.
>
> One of the most important results of metamorphosis relates to eating and food sources. Because of these changes, adult butterflies do not compete for the same food sources with their young. How does this work?
>
> Young butterflies are *larvae*, but we usually call them *caterpillars*. Caterpillars eat leaves. Each species of butterfly has a special "host" plant. The female butterfly lays her eggs only on the leaves of this special plant. That way, when the caterpillars hatch and need to eat, their food source is right there for them.
>
> Adult butterflies do not eat; they only drink their food. Sometimes, the adult butterflies will *puddle*, or gather on moist, sandy soil to drink water. More often, each butterfly drinks nectar through a *proboscis*, the slender "straw" that unfurls from its head.

What butterflies might visit your school grounds? How can you find out what each type of butterfly likes to eat or drink? You can use exploration and experimentation to discover a butterfly's food preferences.

Think about what you would do if you wanted to find out if your friends like hamburgers or pizza best, without asking them. How would you conduct the experiment? You might buy some hamburgers and a pizza. You could put everything on a table and see which food your friends choose to eat. In the same way, we can "set a table" for caterpillars and butterflies. Think about how you might do this.

Directions: Design an experiment that answers the question "What do butterflies like to eat?" Use the *scientific method*: Select the type of butterflies that is native to your area. Make a hypothesis. Research and plan your experiment. Record your observations. Analyze your data and draw a conclusion on the basis of your results.

What Do Baby Swallowtails Swallow?

Directions: Look carefully at swallowtail host plants. Record your observations on the chart below.

Plant	Date planted or date seeds sprout	Date eggs are laid/ number of eggs	Date eggs hatched & number of larvae	Estimate of percentage of plants eaten in one week
Fennel		/		
Parsley		/		
Dill		/		

Note: One way that scientists measure the amount of food that a caterpillar (larva) has eaten is by collecting and weighing *frass*, or caterpillar waste. You may not want to do this, but you can look for green pellets under the plant. If you see *frass* underneath it, then that's where the caterpillar has been eating.

What can you learn from data in the chart?

1. The caterpillars preferred to eat _____ because _____

   _____

   _____

2. If the caterpillars preferred one plant over the others, what does this mean about the other two plants?

   Support your answer. _____

   _____

   _____

3. Fennel and dill are more likely to flower than parsley, but did you notice any butterflies drinking nectar

   from any of these plants? _____ Why do you think they did or did not?

   _____

   _____

CD-104107 *Outdoor Science Classroom*

What Do Adult Swallowtails Swallow?

Directions: Adult butterflies drink flower nectar for their food. See if there is one type of flower that the butterflies like better than others. Observe swallowtail butterflies and complete the chart.
- Record the types of flowers in the first column. Make a mark for each time a butterfly lands on the flower.
- If you see the butterfly's proboscis unfurl, highlight the tally mark using a water-based marker.

Butterfly Visits

Flower	Day 1	Day 2	Day 3	Day 4	Day 5
A					
B					
C					
Example: Marigold	| | |	| |	| | | |	| | | | | | |	| | | | | | |

Think About It! Put yourself in the butterfly's place. Write in the first person (or first insect, to be exact!) to explain the reasons for why you made the choices. (Example: I preferred the nectar of the purple coneflower because . . .) Continue on the back of this page.

_____

_____

_____

_____

_____

_____

_____

_____

_____

_____

© Carson-Dellosa   CD-104107 *Outdoor Science Classroom*

Name: _____   Date: _____

Milk a Weed for All It's Worth!

On most milkweed plants, adult monarch butterflies drink the nectar of the flower. Meanwhile, the caterpillars eat only the leaves on a host plant. This makes for "one-stop shopping" when the monarch is on the go!

Directions: Compare the varieties of milkweed available in your area to find out if monarch butterflies have one they like better than others. Locate three different kinds of milkweed plants if possible. Create a pictograph to track how many times the monarchs visit the plants. Draw a butterfly shape on your graph for every five times the monarchs drink nectar from each kind of milkweed. Observe the milkweed plants over several days. Note: The plant that is most eaten is the favorite variety of the caterpillars.

Sweet Sips

Plant A	🦋 🦋 🦋 🦋 🦋
Plant B	🦋
Plant C	

🦋 = 5 visits

Sweet Sips

Plant A	
Plant B	
Plant C	

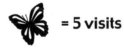 = 5 visits

Results:

Which kind of milkweed should you plant in the school garden? Why?

_____

_____

_____

_____

_____

     CD-104107 *Outdoor Science Classroom*

Name: _____   Date: _____

Raising My Caterpillar

Directions: Take care of a caterpillar that is given to you. Caterpillars only need a small container. There should be tiny pinholes in lid for air, and you must keep the container clean. Clean the caterpillar's home every day. Put in fresh host-plant leaves each day. Complete the sentences below.

1. My caterpillar is the larval stage of a _____ butterfly.
    (species)

2. I got my caterpillar on _____ when it was _____ centimeters long.
    (date)

3. The host plant for this type of caterpillar is _____ .

4. The color of the caterpillar on the first day is _____ .

5. Make a drawing to show how the caterpillar looked on the first day.

6. I predict that the caterpillar will make its chrysalis on _____ .
    (date)

7. After three days, the length of my caterpillar is _____ centimeters.

8. I have made these three observations of my caterpillar in the first three days.
    a. _____
    b. _____
    c. _____

9. I predict my caterpillar will be _____ centimeters long
    in three more days.

Show What You Know: After measuring the growth of your caterpillar every day, make a graph of the growth on the back of this page. Remember to label all parts of the graph.

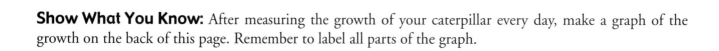

50

Animals Living on the School Grounds

Directions: Find four animals to study. Use this chart to get started.

Animal Characteristics or Adaptations	Animal A _____	Animal B _____	Animal C _____	Animal D _____
Lives in trees				
Able to fly				
Exoskeleton				
Metamorphosis				
Lays eggs				
Cares for young				
Migrates				
Predatory				
Eats only plants				
Humans provide its food				
Swims				
Number of legs				

1. Refer to the chart to sum up what you have learned about animals that live in your area. What do they all have in common? Why? _____

    _____

    _____

2. Which animal do you think is BEST adapted to life in your schoolyard? Why? _____

    _____

    _____

Put It All Together: Divide into groups. Students in each group decide which animal has best adapted for life in the schoolyard. Within your group, work on a presentation for the class. Convince other students that your animal is the best adapted. After the presentations have been given, conduct a survey to see if your classmates have changed their opinions.

Schoolyard Food Chain

A *food chain* represents how energy is passed from plants to animals. In the chain, some animals (called herbivores) feed on plants. Other animals (called carnivores) feed on other animals. Some animals (called omnivores) feed on plants and on other small animals. One animal eats another in order to survive. For example, a food chain in a pond might include a fish that eats algae, a turtle that eats the fish, and a raccoon that eats the turtle. The sun supplies energy to help new algae grow. Then the chain starts all over again.

Directions: Create a diagram in the box below to show a food chain you have seen in the schoolyard. Draw pictures and arrows to show the links in the food chain. Include one plant and three animals. Be sure you have seen at least one of the animals or at least be able to prove there is evidence of that animal living in the area. Label the parts of the food chain: producer, consumer, herbivore, carnivore, and omnivore.

A Food Chain

© Carson-Dellosa

Creative mathematics teachers will tell you that "math is everywhere" and that "you can't teach science without math." When you take students outside, you will find that math really *is* everywhere! Whether it is a geometry lesson using the angles of tree branches or a probability lesson about how many bird eggs will survive to adulthood, math plus science in the outdoors is a winning equation.

The national mathematics standards published by the National Council of Teachers of Mathematics (NCTM) call for students in the earliest grades to begin studying algebra in the form of patterns. What better place than nature to find patterns? Find patterns that occur in the outdoors. Or create a space, such as the math patios described in Chapter One, where students can make patterns and practice skills such as graphing, scale drawing, and keeping a calendar.

Many of the lessons in this chapter are for math patios, but there are also alternatives that might work more easily for you in your schoolyard setting. Some of these alternatives are:

- **String and stakes.** Use small wooden stakes and tie string around them to make a grid. If you have them available, plastic tent stakes are a good alternative. This set-up is one that could be used for a couple of weeks and then dismantled easily.

- **Plywood and tape.** If you cannot have a permanent patio outdoors, make a portable one. Measure equal squares on a plywood board and mark them off with masking tape or duct tape. Store the board when not in use. You can cut the plywood into smaller sections for easy transport to and from the school grounds.

- **Paint on a sidewalk or parking lot.** If your schoolyard is limited in green spaces but heavy on the concrete, mark your grid with tape and then paint it onto the concrete with heavy duty patio paint. Obviously, you'll need permission for this before you start.

- **Jump ropes laid in patterns.** If you have no financial resources for paint, plywood, or string, you could lay jump ropes in a pattern for a single lesson. Any type of rope or yarn will work for a one-time use.

- **Indoor tile floor.** If you cannot take the lesson outdoors, use the tiles on your classroom floor if you have them. Move the desks out of the way and mark the perimeter of your grid.

Each teacher's situation is unique. It takes cooperation among colleagues, administrators, students, and parents to build a permanent outdoor classroom. But one of these alternative ideas will still allow you to put the lessons in this chapter into action for your class, and share the fun of learning on a math grid.

There is a time and a place to break away from traditional presentations of mathematics and make math fun. Let that happen in your outdoor classroom-learning lab, or outside on the school grounds. Integrate math into your outdoor science lessons. It will all add up to success for both you and your students!

CD-104107 *Outdoor Science Classroom*

Teaching with This Chapter

There are several ways you can use the lessons in this chapter. You may wish to use some lessons to meet a math objective, while others can be used as an extension of science or social studies lessons. Link science content to math concepts by explaining how various scientists use math skills in their work. On some lessons, the type of scientist who uses the skill from the activity is listed along with the objectives. Handouts for the activities start on page 61.

Hunting for Numbers

Teaching Objective: To identify a variety of numbers in nature; to practice basic mathematics operations

Scientists Who Use These Skills: biologists

Materials: handout, clipboard, pencil, paper or plastic grocery bags

Procedures and Tips: This activity is an old-fashioned scavenger hunt in which students practice percentages, addition, and subtraction. Give each student a plastic grocery bag and the handout. Tell them they are going on a hunt for the items on the handout and ask them to predict how many they will find. Ask them to put each item they find into their grocery bag.

If you are certain several of the items listed on the handout cannot be found in your area, you may want to modify the chart. But leave those items if you want to let that fact work into the percentages the students are predicting. This would also help them to think about the environmental factors and seasonal changes that may influence which items are present and which are not.

Think about conducting this activity close to the beginning of the school year as an introduction to the outdoor classroom. Make sure that when students have finished the activity, all of their natural items are returned to nature.

Graphing Animal Behavior

Teaching Objective: To gather data to include in a bar graph; to use science and math skills together; to observe animal behavior in nature

Scientists Who Use These Skills: biologists

Materials: concrete block patio, animals in natural setting, handout, pencil

Procedures and Tips: The aim of this lesson is to help students see the relationship between science and math. Students will produce both a written graph and a "human bar graph", using the data they have gathered from their scientific observations of schoolyard animals.

Take time to scout the schoolyard for animal activities. Birds will likely be the most easily observed animals in many places. To increase their activity, provide a number of special treats when you plan to conduct this activity. Temporary feeders can be created from clay flower-pot saucers filled with seeds, pine cones rolled in peanut butter and seeds, or gallon milk jugs cut with a large hole and filled with seeds. Put one of these on a stump or near a tree. The feeders will probably also attract squirrels, which can then be observed as well. Or, you can observe insects. The number of times a bee or a butterfly visits a flower will create good data for a graph.

Teaching with This Chapter

Allow your students to gather data for a half-hour or so each day for a week. Then ask them to draw a graph in the box provided on the handout. Students should label their graphs with numbers and descriptors of the animal behavior measured. Ask to see each completed graph to make sure data is recorded correctly.

After each student has a graph, have them take turns organizing their classmates to make the human graph. Help them come up with a method to make the graph workable. For example, each person in a line could represent five times that birds came to a certain bird feeder.

What's Your Net Worth?

Teaching Objective: To practice measurement skills; to design an experiment to test the effectiveness of an insect net

Materials: wooden dowel, duct tape, wire clothes hanger, wire snips, roll of fabric mesh, fishing line, tape measure, large dull needle and heavy thread, handout, clipboard, pencil

Procedures and Tips: Your students can build a butterfly net with simple materials from home or a hardware store. Then they can measure their own net and compare it to other student's nets. Make sure students make their nets with dowels of different lengths, and nets of different sizes, to aid in comparisons.

Follow this procedure for making a insect net:

1. Cut the hook off the clothes hanger and untwist the top.

2. Shape the wire into a circle, leaving enough straight wire to go alongside the dowel about 25 centimeters.

3. Wrap duct tape around the wire and dowel to secure the wire circle.

4. Measure how much fabric mesh you will need to go around the wire circle.

5. Secure the fabric to the wire circle by tying it with fishing line. It can be tied in small knots or sewn all the way around and down the open edge with the needle and thread.

After the nets are complete, your class should take the measurements shown on the student handout diagram. As an additional math activity, students can calculate the cost of their nets—provide them with a list of prices based on receipts for the supplies.

Allow students to use their nets to catch butterflies and other flying insects. Then gather information on the size of each net built in the class and the number of insects caught by that net. Find out if there are certain patterns of success that relate to the sizes of the nets. Finally, have students graph the results.

Teaching with This Chapter

What Can You Learn from a Seed?

Teaching Objective: To practice measurement and percentages; to germinate a seed and make quantitative observations

Materials: seeds or dried beans, paper towels, resealable plastic bags, water, metric ruler, digital scale or balance scale, container and potting soil or garden space (optional)

Procedures and Tips: Growing seeds is a common science activity in many classrooms, but it is also an effective mathematics lesson.

Dried beans from the grocery store are easy to use for this activity because they are big and easy for children to handle, weigh, and measure. If you prefer to grow flowers, buy sunflower seeds. For a larger vegetable seed, think about planting pumpkins.

Make sure you have metric rulers marked in millimeters and centimeters. Weighing the seeds may be a little trickier than measuring length, depending on your scale. A high-quality digital scale works best, but nearly any scale from a science kit will do. If one seed does not weigh enough to make the scale register a number, ask the students what they should do. With encouragement, they will come up with the idea of weighing the entire package of seeds and dividing the weight by the number in the bag.

Students will germinate the seeds in plastic bags. Ask them to moisten their paper towels lightly after folding the seed gently inside, and to place the towel in the resealable bag. Keep the bags near a window, but not in direct sunlight. As the days pass, watch the plants sprout, and follow the questions on the handout with your students.

When the seedlings are getting close to outgrowing the bag, you may wish to provide a planting space outdoors or in a container. Otherwise, send the seedlings home and ask students to plant them in their own yards or gardens. This is also a good way to get parents involved in math and science instruction!

Germination Determination! Old Seeds, New Seeds

Teaching Objective: To compare and contrast the germination rates of seeds produced for different years; to create a line graph based on data gathered in an experiment

Materials: two or more packets of seeds for the same plant, each produced during a different year; outdoor garden spot or pots and potting soil for indoors; water source for plants; pencil; handouts; clipboard; craft sticks for plant markers

Procedures and Tips: Many stores will give teachers seeds at the end of the summer-growing season. If you can collect these packets about the time the school year starts, you can buy new seeds in the spring and have the two years' worth of seeds for this experiment.

Follow this procedure for the activity:

1. Plant the seeds from two different years under identical circumstances. For ease in mathematics calculations, choose 10 seeds to plant from each year's packet.

Teaching with This Chapter

2. If planting in pots, use identical pots and measure the amount of potting soil so it is equal.

3. Plant the seeds according to package instructions, usually just below the surface.

4. Label the pots with plant markers to show the type of plant and year of seeds.

5. Make predictions and gather data. Use the handouts.

Students should fill in the chart as the seeds are growing. The second handout is a culminating activity in which students create a line graph comparing the seeds from two different years. This can be done as a whole-class activity with only two flower pots of seeds, one from each year's seed packet.

If you are looking for a good source of seeds, apply for a grant at www.kidsgardening.com and you will receive a variety of seeds in the mail.

It's About Time & Human Sundial

Teaching Objective: To use the sun to measure time; to practice measuring distance

Scientists Who Use These Skills:
anthropologists, naturalists

Materials: paper plates, straws, tape, pencil, pattern, compass, handouts

Procedures and Tips: First, have students research the history of telling time. Next, give students the handout (see page 67) and ask them to answer the background questions and write a hypothesis about how to make a sundial. Then give them the materials and let them make sundials.

Take students outside on a sunny day to test their creations. Check the sundials with a watch. You will need to decide how to manage getting outdoors on the hour for multiple hours, so consider sharing this activity with another teacher. If you are a departmentalized science or math teacher, it should be fairly easy to take out groups of students to mark different hours.

When marking shadows, students use the straw as a gnomon (or shadow caster). They will need to lean the straw slightly toward North (the angle of the gnomon depends on your latitude). If you don't have a compass available, look on a local map or use a car that has an electronic compass to find the direction of true North. After your students have made a shadow on the plate with the straw gnomon, use your watch to help them indicate the time with an hour line.

If you want to extend this experience, make a human sundial following this procedure:

1. Explain how to make a human sundial. For example: "You and your classmates can make a human sundial. A *gnomon* is the part of a sundial that casts the shadow. On the individual sundials you made, the straw was the gnomon. On this sundial, a person will act as the gnomon."

2. Have students make a mark on the ground in a sunny space. You may want to use a brick or concrete block so the mark does not move easily. If you want to do this activity on a paved area, you can mark your spot with chalk.

3. Find the direction North. Draw a line straight out from the student (gnomon), as she stands on the spot you marked, toward North. This line will be noon. Try to go outdoors at noon to test the mark on the ground.

4. Make other marks by having students stand on the spot every hour on the hour. It may take you several days to complete this. You can lay out boards or tie string or yarn to stakes to help you mark the hours. Have students take turns with their classmates and let everyone have a chance to cast a shadow. You may want to divide into groups and make several human sundials.

Be an Archaeologist! Make a Grid

Teaching Objective: To practice making use of a scaled drawing; to use a grid to measure the distance between objects in a mock dig site

Scientists Who Use These Skills: archaeologists, paleontologists

Materials: For part one—handout, metric ruler, pencil; For part two—meterstick, yardstick, or tape measure, play sand from local home improvement store, landscape timbers, nails, string, landscape plastic, heavy duty stapler, clay "artifacts"

Procedures and Tips: Guide students in a discussion about why scientists working on an archaeological dig would need math skills. You may wish to have students research a current archaeological dig on the Internet so that they can visualize the techniques employed. Sometimes you can find a site with real-time video streaming. After you have thoroughly discussed the math needs of archaeologists, give students the handout and have them work on the exercises.

Extend the lesson in a long-term project by having students help you build a mock dig site in which they can practice the skills of using a grid. Read more about this outdoor activity in Chapter 1.

Follow this procedure for the activity:

1. Determine the size of the area using the meterstick or tape measure.

2. Build an edge around the perimeter with landscape timbers.

3. Line the area with landscape grade plastic, and staple the plastic to the interior edge of the timbers.

4. Use a nail to poke random holes in the plastic to allow potential rainwater to drain.

5. Fill the plastic with sand to a depth of about 30 centimeters, or use enough sand to cover potential "artifacts" you would like to hide.

6. Buy plastic bone sets from a dollar store or a science company catalogue. Buy clay pots to hide as well. The bones may be separated and buried, and the pots may be broken and buried.

7. Have students use small trowels, brushes, and other tools to remove enough sand to determine the location of the "artifacts."

8. Put nails evenly spaced in the landscape timbers and run a string grid over the dig so that students can sketch a scaled drawing of where each item has been found.

9. Items may be retrieved, and students may work in groups to rebuild skeletons or pots.

Teaching with This Chapter

Measuring Erosion and Analyzing Erosion

Teaching Objective: To apply use of measurement skills; to recognize the effects of water erosion on land

Scientists Who Use These Skills: landscape architects

Materials: meterstick or measuring tapes, flag markers, clipboard, handouts, pencil, calculators

Procedures and Tips: This is an activity that can be done indoors or outdoors, but if weather produces erosion in your schoolyard, that is the ideal location for this lesson. Scout your schoolyard for even the slightest slope, and look for evidence of erosion and deposition. Make sure your administrator knows what you are doing and approves of your students observing the erosion in a particular place. If he or she resists, offer to have your students propose solutions to erosion problems on the school grounds.

Once you obtain permission, students can gather data from the area of erosion. Follow this procedure:

1. Find an area where erosion has begun. Mark both sides of the gully with a flag (you can purchase builders' mark flags at hardware store). Make sure the flags are firmly in the ground.

2. Measure the width from flag to flag by laying a meterstick straight across the gully.

3. Measure the depth by leaving the meterstick in place, and measuring down from the meterstick to the deepest spot in the gully. If you wish to measure deposition, place a plastic or metal ruler in the ground in the location where the soil is gathering.

4. Record your observations.

5. Repeat at regular intervals following rain showers.

6. Analyze your results.

Help the students complete the handouts with appropriate numbers. You may wish to have different classes work in different areas of the schoolyard for comparison. *Variation:* If you need to do the activity indoors, use an under-the-bed plastic container filled with soil or sand. Put it on the floor with one end propped up on blocks or a brick. Pour a controlled amount of water on it each day for a week. Gather your results each day, and have students use the handout as with the outdoor version of the activity.

Weather or Not

Teaching Objective: To average a group of numbers; to make a scientific prediction

Scientists Who Use These Skills: meteorologists

Materials: outdoor thermometer, rain gauge (available from most garden centers)

Procedures and Tips: This lesson will help students recognize that meteorologists are scientists who use math skills. You may wish to invite a weather forecaster from a local television station to speak to your students. Opening this lesson with a real meteorologist, whether recorded or live can help your students think the way a scientist thinks. If that is not possible, look for a video on weather, or tape a short segment from a weather forecast to share with your students as an introduction.

Students will be watching weather forecasts to gather data on weather predictions for the week.

But they will be recording the air temperature and precipitation measurements at school. The best place to place a thermometer is in a grassy area at least 2 meters from the building or concrete surfaces. This will help avoid having the air temperature affected by the transfer of heat energy from these surfaces.

Students should complete the chart and graph the information according to instructions on the handout. As a culminating activity, you may want to use a video camera and have students record their own weather show complete with data from their experiments and predictions for the coming days. Your school may allow you to show this on a closed circuit television system if it is available.

Math in a Tree

Teaching Objective: To practice measuring angles, circumference, and diameter

Scientists Who Use These Skills: arborists, foresters

Materials: tape measure, meterstick or ruler, clear protractor, handout, clipboard, pencil

Procedures and Tips: This is an exercise in using the tools of mathematics as students take measurements of trees in the schoolyard. The activity could be used as an introduction to measurement, as a mid-point practice, or as a culminating activity after a unit on measurement is under way. You can have the class do this activity in any season, but you may want to think about late fall as an ideal time. At that point of the year, there will be a variety of leaves on the ground for the leaf comparison, and foliage should be thin enough to make measuring angles of branches easier. Although this is a simple lesson, it shows the direct connections between math and science. Scientists are interested in the density of trees for a number of reasons. The health of a forest can be judged by some of these measurements, which is why forest rangers would use them. As scientists try to preserve natural lands, they may want to help limit development. Providing builders with a required density of trees per square kilometer could be helpful in such a preservation effort. Lead a discussion about the practical value of making these measurements.

Simple Machines Are for the Birds

Teaching Objective: To design an experiment using simple machines; to practice using percentages

Scientists Who Use These Skills: ornithologists, engineers

Materials: birdfeeder, small buckets, seed, funnel, pulley, rope, boards, screws/nails, hammer, screwdriver, handout, pencil

Procedures and Tips: Students will use measurement skills to design an invention that fills a bird feeder with seeds. Start by handing out the reproducible and discuss with your students the different uses of simple machines in everyday life. A hammer, for instance, is both a lever and a wedge. A butter knife is a wedge. Ask them to think of other examples. Discuss which simple machines might work the best for filling a bird feeder.

You can do this activity as a demonstration if you only have one bird feeder. That would be the most cost-effective way to attempt this lesson. Position the funnel in the top of the bird feeder so that the seeds will have a fair chance of dropping into the feeder.

Teaching with This Chapter

This is truly an experiment, so give your students the freedom to try some things that do not work. That is how real scientists experiment, and that is what will yield the numbers your students will manipulate on the second part of the handout.

Whatever your students design, they should be able to handle the simple machine, and let it pour seed into the funnel and bird feeder. Discuss how one practical use of a successful machine would be to fill feeders that are out of reach. This would allow feeders to be placed higher up in trees, away from many predators of birds.

One simple machine that filled bird feeders successfully in the past was an inclined plane that took the seeds up above the feeder with a conveyor (the conveyor took additional materials that included lumber, a plastic handle, and rubber matting). Another successful machine made with materials listed for this activity included a pulley and rope lifting a bucket above the funnel and a second rope that pulled on the bucket to tip it.

Building and Using a Compost Bin

Teaching Objective: To practice using measurement skills; to read a thermometer accurately

Scientists Who Use These Skills: botanists, food scientists

Materials for Building: wire fencing (hog wire or chicken wire); six pieces of pretreated lumber 2 inches x 4 inches x 8 feet; nails; hammer; saw; heavy-duty carpenter's stapler

Materials for Activities: long thermometers, food scraps, yard scraps, handout, clipboard, pencil

Procedures and Tips: Build a compost bin with your students and use it to recycle fruit and vegetable scraps as well as yard waste into valuable compost for your school garden.

To make the bins: Cut each board into two 4-foot lengths. Use nails to fasten the 12 boards into a 4 feet x 4 feet x 4 feet frame. Use a carpenter's stapler to affix the wire fencing to the four vertical sides of the cube. You may leave the top open or use a piece of plywood as a cover. (If the compost bin is uncovered, it will work, but be sure to check your local ordinances to see if a cover is required by law.)

Place the bin about 30 feet (10 meters) away from the school building if possible. The bin may attract insects. Some compost bins emit an odor, but you can avoid that by limiting the waste you put in it and stirring often. Use apple cores, banana peels, or scraps from a school salad bar. Never include animal byproducts in your compost. Gardening scraps can be included, e.g., clippings from flowers and shrubs. Layers should alternate, as the food scraps will hasten the decomposition of the yard waste. Also, keep the materials in the compost bin damp by adding water whenever necessary.

One way to test the compost bin for effectiveness is to determine the temperature inside the heap. Some science classrooms are equipped with long thermometers which your students can stick through the wire and into the heap as far as possible. The compost heap should show an internal temperature several degrees higher than the air temperature. Try taking the bin's temperature at different times during the day, or every day for a week at the same time. These numbers can be represented on a graph drawn on the math patio blocks of your outdoor classroom!

Hunting for Numbers

Directions: You're on a hunt for the items you see below! Mark the square in the chart with a check mark when you have found the set of items. Put the items in your grocery bag. If you find everything, bring the bag to your teacher to be checked. When you are finished, answer the questions below the chart.

Before you start hunting, read through the whole chart and predict how many items you think you can find.

Prediction: I will find _____ of the 20 sets of items.

3 acorns	7 sticks	4 rocks	2 leaves from the same tree	10 flower petals
1 ivy leaf	6 brown leaves	5 weeds	8 different leaves	2 seeds
4 pinecones	1 maple seed	2 oak tree leaves	6 dandelions	1 wildflower
9 pieces of fallen bark	4 feathers	1 snail shell	12 blades of grass	11 pine needles

1. Add each vertical column. Add all of the numbers including those items you did not find. Write your answers below the columns.

2. On the back of this paper, write five challenging word problems using these numbers and items for friends to solve.

3. What percentage of the total items (20) did you find? Count each set of items as 1 for this question.

4. Work with a partner. What is the difference in the percentage of items each of you found? If you combined your charts, what would the new percentage of found items be?

Graphing Animal Behavior

Directions: On your hundreds-chart patio, or a grid of 10 x 10 squares, graph the data about an animal's behavior. You can use the data from other charts you have completed or you can collect new data. The amount or type of food a butterfly or bird eats is easy to graph.

Getting Started: First, make a *hypothesis*, a prediction that can be tested with experiments or observations. For example, your hypothesis might be "Hummingbirds like nectar from flowers better than sugar water from a hummingbird feeder." Watch the animal over a period of time and record your data. Here's a sample of what your chart might look like

Sample Data Gathered

Day	Number of times hummingbirds come to flowers	Number of times hummingbirds come to feeder
Monday	3	4
Tuesday	1	1
Wednesday	2	3
Thursday	0	6
Friday	1	5
Total	7	19

Graph It! Use your data and turn your patio into a "human bar graph." If you were using the sample above, make two columns for Monday. Ask three classmates to stand in column one, and four classmates to stand in column two. By the time you place students in a column for every day and for the preferred food source, the whole class will be involved!

More Graphing! Gather paper, a pencil and a ruler. Using the data you collected during this experiment, make a bar graph on paper to represent your results. Label the graph clearly and give it an appropriate title.

© Carson-Dellosa   CD-104107 *Outdoor Science Classroom*

Name: _____   Date: _____

What's Your Net Worth?
Measuring and Using an Insect Net

Directions: Answer the questions about your insect net. You will need a meterstick.

Measurements:

1. The length of my net's handle is _____ cm.

2. The circumference (distance around the opening)

   of my net's hoop is _____ cm.

3. The diameter (distance across the opening) of my net's hoop is _____ cm.

4. The depth of the actual net from hoop to bottom of the inside is _____ cm.

Success Rate:

5. While using the net outdoors, I attempted to catch _____ insects,

   and I actually caught _____ of them.

6. The percentage of those I caught was _____ .

Compare and Contrast: After collecting insects, work with a partner to answer the questions.

7. Whose net caught more butterflies or other insects? _____

8. Why do you think this net caught more?

9. On another sheet of paper, make a bar graph to compare the size and results of the two nets. Graph at least four sets of numbers. Then make a conclusion about what makes a good insect net on the basis of your results.

CD-104107 *Outdoor Science Classroom*

Name: _____   Date: _____

What Can You Learn from a Seed?

Have you ever planted a seed? If so, what kind of seed? What did you learn from it? Get a seed from your teacher. Examine it carefully. Predict how the seed will change. You will be amazed at all that you can learn from one tiny seed!

Day 1

1. The weight of my seed is _____ grams.
   If my seed were too light to weigh, I would calculate the weight by _____.

2. The length of my seed is _____ millimeters.

3. I predict my seed will become a _____.
                                                    (type of plant)
In order to be able to measure your seed again, you will start to grow it on a damp paper towel inside a plastic sandwich bag. Your teacher will show you how to do this. You will measure it again in three days. Predict how much you think it will grow by then.

4. I think my seed will weigh _____ grams and be _____ centimeters long in three days.

Day 4

1. My seed (and the plant, if it is started) weighs _____ grams. The difference between this weight and my prediction is _____ grams.

2. My seed (and plant) is _____ centimeters long. The difference between this length and my prediction is _____ centimeters.

3. Find the percentage of growth that took place. For example, if you predicted your seed would weigh 10 grams and it weighs 9 grams, then 90% of the growth in weight that you predicted took place. Figure an answer for both weight and length. Average the two percentages.

4. Work in a group of three students. How do the actual results compare with each person's predictions? Were they close? Make a bar graph to compare the predictions and actually measurements. Choose a speaker from your group to share your results with the class.

Follow-up: Plant your seeds in a pot or outdoors in a garden. You can make more predictions and see what happens to your plant. After your seedling is planted in dirt, measure the height from the ground to the top of the plant. Do this every day for 14 days. Make a line graph to represent the data you collected.

   CD-104107 *Outdoor Science Classroom*

Germination Determination!
Old Seeds, New Seeds

Have you ever read a seed package carefully? Have you noticed that seed packages have a date stamped on them? The date is the year during which the seeds should be planted. Some people still plant seeds that more than a year old and other people discard the seeds.

Directions: *Germination,* the growth of a seedling from a seed, can be tested in this simple experiment. Work in pairs. One person plants the older seeds. The other person plants the newer seeds. As your plants grow, fill in the chart below or your own chart on another sheet of paper. Make a conclusion about your results and answer the questions.

Data Chart:

Date	Quantitative Data*	Comments or Observations
Ex.: planted 09-01-05	10/05 sunflowers, 10/04 sunflowers	Seeds look the same.
Ex.: 09-08-05	10/05 flowers at 6 cm or more	Stems and leaves are green; only difference is in height
	10/04 flowers at 4 cm or less	

* Data that is *quantitative* is noted in numbers, such as weight, height, length, etc.

1. What happened to your seeds during the first week? How did they change?

_____

_____

2. Explain the difference in the growth of plants from new seeds and older ones.

_____

_____

3. Think about the result. Would you plant old seeds during the next year? Why or why not?

_____

_____

It's About Time!
Sundial Activity

Materials: Paper plate, drinking straw, tape or modeling clay, pencil, pattern (see page 68), compass

Directions: Gather your materials and complete the steps below.

1. Write a hypothesis that proposes how you could make a sundial.

If . . . _____,

then . . . _____.

2. Using the materials listed above, make a paper-plate sundial. Your sundial can be constructed any way you want, as long as you believe it will work.

3. Test your sundial in a sunny place outdoors. Face the dial North, and use the straw to cast a shadow. Mark the hour on the face of your sundial in pencil. You can test it again at the same time during two other days to check its accuracy.

4. Draw a picture of your sundial at work.

5. Mark the other times on the sundial.
What percentage of accuracy do you think your sundial has?

Think About It!

1. How do people today measure the time when they do not have a watch or clock?

2. Before the clock was invented, how did people measure time?

3. How could you make an accurate sundial if you were in the wilderness?

Sundial Pattern

Directions: Use this pattern to lay out your sundial on a paper plate. Cut out the pieces. Glue them in place after testing your sundial and comparing your marks to the time on a watch. The shadows cast by the sun is specific to your location. Take the sundial outside to check it every hour on the hour. You may have to spend a few minutes doing this each day for a week.

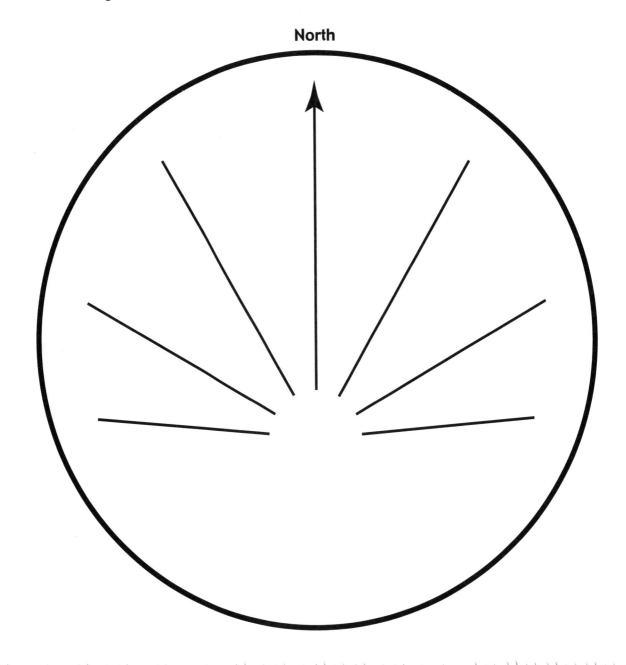

North

Make a Human Sundial

Directions: Work with your class and follow your teacher's instructions to make a human sundial. Test the human sundial against the paper-plate sundial. Compare the results and answer the questions below.

1. At noon, in what direction is your shadow casted?

2. How many minutes' difference is there in the accuracy of the two sundials?

3. Which sundial is more accurate? Why?

4. In what ways is the shadow of the human sundial the same or different during different times of the day?

5. Are the angles between each hour the same? Explain.

6. How is a sundial the same and different from a traditional clock?

7. Make a third sundial by sticking a twig in the ground. Let the twig cast a shadow. Could you do this if you were in the wilderness and needed to know the time? Describe what you would do. What materials would you need if the sky was overcast?

                                    CD-104107 *Outdoor Science Classroom*

Name: _____   Date: _____

Be an Archaeologist!
Make a Grid

Directions: When an archaeologist digs up artifacts, the scientist must carefully make a record of where the artifacts were found. This helps each scientist to reconstruct the past accurately. See if you can make mathematical sense of this scientific discovery. The space between the lines represents an actual space of 10 centimeters. Draw the strings that would go horizontally and vertically over the dig. The grid over the dig site represents one made of string and stakes. Using the key, answer the questions below.

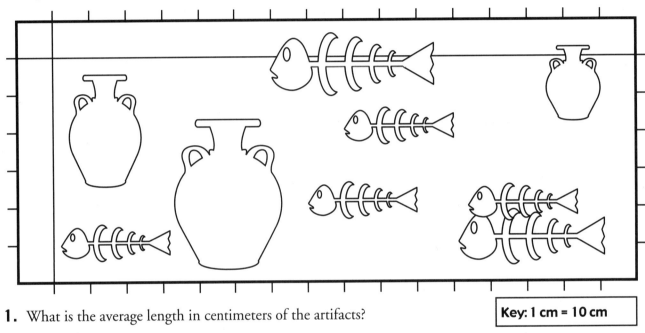

Key: 1 cm = 10 cm

1. What is the average length in centimeters of the artifacts?

2. What is the height and width of each pot?

3. What are some possible explanations for why the artifacts and pots ended up in this pattern? Pretend you are the scientist who made this discovery. Write a journal entry and tell the events of the past that led to the layout of this find. Write your entry on the back of this page.

More Digging! Working with a team of three or four students, set up an archaeological dig in your outdoor classroom area for other students to investigate.

Measuring Erosion

Erosion, the movement of soil caused by water or wind, can be easily observed in the schoolyard. You can also measure *deposition,* the deposit of soil after it has been eroded.

Directions: Follow the local weather and choose some days that rain is predicted. Be patient, and you will be able to observe the mighty force of erosion! Be sure to make accurate marks when measuring the ground with a meterstick or measuring tape and keep exact records. Fill in the blanks below.

Date of First Observation: _____

1. The original width of the eroded gully is _____ cm.

2. The original depth of the eroded gully is _____ cm.

3. An area of deposition is identified: Yes _____   No _____

Date of Second Observation: _____

1. Width _____ cm **2.** Depth _____ cm **3.** Deposition depth _____ cm

Date of Third Observation: _____

1. Width _____ cm **2.** Depth _____ cm **3.** Deposition depth _____ cm

Date of Fourth Observation: _____

1. Width _____ cm **2.** Depth _____ cm **3.** Deposition depth _____ cm

4. Draw a picture of the gully on the back of this page.

                    CD-104107 *Outdoor Science Classroom*

Analyzing Erosion Measurements

Directions: Now that you have gathered data on erosion, what does it mean? Can you draw conclusions about the erosion that you observed? You need to look at all of the information you have gathered. Put it into the graph below. You may use the grid below for a line graph. Be sure to label the graph properly. (If you have a math patio outdoors, you can draw your graph on the patio with sidewalk chalk.)

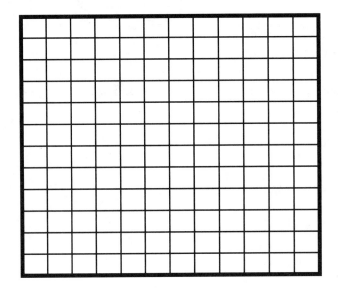

1. Look at your graph. What trend does it show in the erosion? Does the deposition change in the same way? Is it what you thought it would be? How did the amount of rain affect the erosion? Write a paragraph about your observations. Make sure your paragraph clearly explains the information on your graph.

_____

_____

_____

_____

_____

2. Use your drawing of the gully from the activity Measuring Erosion. Add arrows and words to show how the area changed from the first time you observed it.

   CD-104107 *Outdoor Science Classroom*

Name: _____   Date: _____

Weather or Not

How do we talk about weather? Do we use only words to describe weather, or does it take more? Of course it does! Numbers help us measure the weather and the way it affects us. In this activity, you'll take some measurements and make some observations just like a *meteorologist,* a scientist who studies atmospheric conditions and makes weather predictions.

Materials: thermometer, rain gauge, weather reports (television, newspaper, or Internet)

Directions: Watch a television weather forecast or read newspaper or Internet weather reports. Look at what high air temperatures and rainfall are predicted for this week. Using everything you have learned, make your own prediction about the high temperature and the amount of rainfall for each day. Record your predictions in the chart below. In order to make measurements for the second week of this activity, place a thermometer and rain gauge on your school grounds. If this is not possible, read or listen to weather reports to get your data.

	Monday	**Tuesday**	**Wednesday**	**Thursday**	**Friday**
Forecast for Week 1 Temp. / Rain	Ex. 72 degrees / 1 inch				
YOUR prediction for Week 2					
Actual numbers for Week 2					

Analyze the Data:

1. What was the average difference between your prediction and the actual air temperature?

2. What is the relationship between the amount of rain and the temperature? Use math concepts to explain your theory.

3. What was the total rainfall amount for the Week 2? What total did you predict?

4. On the other side of this sheet, write a word problem that requires a prediction for another week, based on your data from this week. Copy your word problem onto another piece of paper and trade with a classmate. Check each others' work and help make any corrections needed.

Math in a Tree

Directions: Math is everywhere in the great outdoors. You can add it all up by finding the sum of math in a tree. First, choose a tree on your school grounds or nearby park. Then answer the following questions about that tree.

Materials:
   Tape measure
   Meterstick/ruler
   Clear protractor

1. What is the circumference of the trunk 20 centimeters up from the ground? 50 centimeters up? Next, lay your tape measure on the ground in a circle to show each measurement. What is the diameter of each measurement?

   Circumference 20 cm up _____ cm   Diameter _____ cm

   Circumference 50 cm up _____ cm   Diameter _____ cm

2. Find a branch that you can either reach or see clearly. Look through your protractor at the branch. Measure the angle of the branch to the tree. Repeat this step with another branch. If these two angles were part of a triangle, what would the measurement of the third angle in the triangle be?

   1st tree angle _____   2nd tree angle _____

   Remaining angle needed to complete a triangle: _____

3. Find four different-sized leaves from your tree. Find the average of their lengths and widths. What is the average size of a leaf from your tree?

   Average Length _____ cm   Average Width _____ cm

4. Look carefully at your tree. Back up a little from it. Estimate the height of your tree.

   I estimate the tree is _____ meters tall.

Simple Machines Are for the Birds

Use your measurement skills to design an invention that fills a bird feeder with seeds. This is a discovery activity. You will need to experiment with the materials to find a design that works. There is no "right or wrong" way to design your invention. Be creative!

Hypothesis: If I use one or more simple machines to invent a bird-feeder filler, I can put 30 grams of birdseed in a feeder using only my invention.

Materials: bird feeder, birdseed, funnel, pulley, rope, boards, wood screws and or nail, hammer, screwdriver, small bucket, metric ruler, scale

Background: There are six types of simple machines: screw, pulley, inclined plane, wheel and axle, wedge, and lever. They are designed to make work easier for us. When two or more of these are combined, they become a complex machine. Using the materials you have, design an invention that makes filling a bird feeder easier.

Simple Machines:

Look at the pictures of simple machines below. Think of two other examples for each category and write those names in the blanks. On the back of this paper, draw two examples for the wheel-and-axle category.

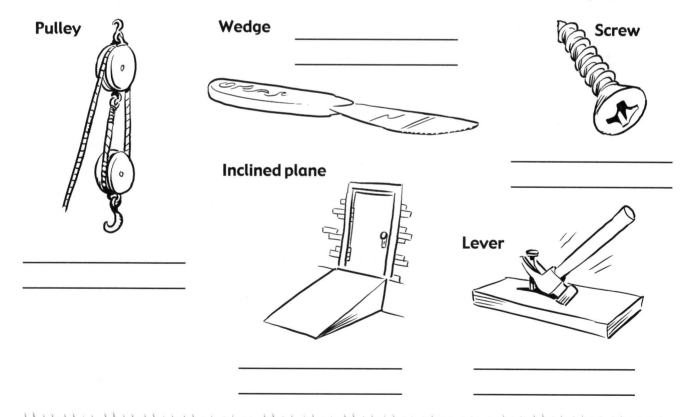

Pulley

Wedge _____

_____

Screw

_____

Inclined plane

_____

Lever

_____ _____

CD-104107 *Outdoor Science Classroom*

Simple Machines
Are for the Birds

Directions: Follow the steps below.

1. Make a sketch of how you plan to put your materials together to fill the feeder. Label each side of your machine with its measurement in centimeters. Use arrows and captions to show your invention in action.

2. Now you will test your invention. Answer the questions below after you have tried using your invention three times.

Directions: Record your data and answer the questions.

1. What measurements did you need to make as you put your invention together? (wood, rope, etc.)

2. How much birdseed (in grams) actually dropped into the bird feeder on each of your three tries?

   1st_____   2nd_____   3rd_____

3. What percentage of the total amount of seeds made it into the bird feeder each time?

   1st_____   2nd_____   3rd_____

4. Was the hypothesis correct? Were you able to fill the feeder by using simple machines?

5. What changes would you like to make to your bird-feeder filler to improve its accuracy?

Building and Using a Compost Bin

Directions: Is there math in a compost bin? You bet there is! Find out what's "cooking" inside. Use a thermometer to find the difference between the temperature inside the compost and the air temperature outside of the bin. Complete the steps below and record your data.

1. Finish the prediction: I think the temperature in the compost bin is (**lower   higher   same**) as the temperature outside.

2. Measure the temperature inside the bin and the air temperature outside of the bin. Complete the chart below. Record the temperature every hour or at the same time every day. *Note:* When you are measuring the heat of the compost, push the thermometer into the compost heap as far as it will go.

Temperature

	Day / Hour 1	Day / Hour 2	Day / Hour 3	Day / Hour 4	Day / Hour 5
Inside the compost bin					
Outside of compost bin					

Directions: On another sheet of paper, answer the following questions.

3. Is there a pattern in the temperature readings? Make a graph to represent the data.

4. What were the results of your temperature experiment? Is the temperature inside the compost bin generally cooler or warmer than the outside air? Why?

5. Write a paragraph describing your findings and your conclusion. Tell how you think heat energy plays a role in decomposition.

6. What would you do differently if you did the experiment again?

Reading and Writing About Nature

The integration of science and language arts is an effective way that teachers can enhance the comprehension/critical thinking of the students and the requirements of their curriculum. Both writing and reading can be readily emphasized during science lessons. When students write about what they learn in science, it reinforces the science concepts and allows them to practice writing skills that they will be using across the curriculum. Most students love to learn about wildlife, so reading about wild animals and nature is a high-interest way to engage students in using reading strategies during science class periods.

When selecting writing assignments related to the outdoors, think about outdoor lessons that have sparked the most interest from your students. If possible, find a nature journal written by a scientist and read an example to them. Some journals show how scientists and naturalists use text, sketches and measurements to record sightings of unfamiliar plants or animals, which students often find fascinating.

Reading materials related to the outdoors are plentiful. A great read-aloud in your outdoor classroom that's about an outdoor topic can be powerful. Sometimes it can even be followed up indoors with a clip from a movie. One of the best sources for teachers is the National Science Teachers Association & Children's Book Council annual list titled "Outstanding Science Trade Books for Children." These books have been reviewed by teachers and carefully screened for quality. You can find several years' worth of these lists on the Internet at www.nsta.org. Media specialists often order every book on this list, so check to see if your school has them.

There are many alternatives to fire the imaginations of your students and while you weave together science and language arts activities. Here are just a few of those alternatives:

- Read several books about wetland environments. Then set up an aquarium in the classroom to contain a wetland ecosystem. For example, you could have water plants, minnows, snails, and a small water turtle in your aquarium. Students can keep journals about their observations.

- Read an ecological mystery, such as *Who Really Killed Cock Robin?* Then set up a mystery in your outdoor classroom for your students to solve. "Plant" evidence, such as a bird nest on the ground, some feathers, or an empty turtle shell. Encourage students to write their own mystery story that connects and explains the "clues."

- After reading a migration story, such as *Fly Away Home* by Patricia Hermes, locate the migration routes of Canada geese. Find a town with a school near one of the main routes. Use an Internet directory to locate the school's address. Write a class letter to the students there, asking them to write to you when the Canada geese migrate to their home. The book *Fly Away Home* is a novelization of the movie by the same name, not to be confused by Eve Bunting's story.

- Read an essay by John Muir or another naturalist. Then turn the essay into a play that your class can perform on Earth Day.

Enjoy reading and writing outdoors with your kids. Their enthusiasm might even inspire you to write your own creative science-related work!

CD-104107 *Outdoor Science Classroom*

Reading Suggestions

Nothing makes the science-reading connection in a stronger way than a really good book. Here are some suggestions for books in the classroom that your students will enjoy for both their wonderful writing and their science content.

Title	Author	Publisher	ISBN
Mathematics			
Ten Seeds	Ruth Brown	Knopf Random House	0375806970
Nature's Paintbrush: Patterns and Colors Around You	Susan Stockdale	Simon & Schuster	0689810814
Butterfly Count	Sneed B. Collard, III	Holiday House	0823416070
Paleontology/Archaeology			
The Magic School Bus: Lost in the Time of Dinosaurs	Joanna Cole	Scholastic	0590446894
Science K–3			
Birds Build Nests	Yvonne Winer	Charlesbridge	1570915008
Butterflies in the Garden	Carol Lerner	HarperCollins	0688174787
Butternut Hollow Pond	Brian Hienz	Millbrook Press	0761313257
Science Grades 4–7			
The Talking Earth	Jean Craighead George	HarperCollins	0064402126
I Want to be an Environmentalist	Stephanie Maze	Harcourt	015201862X
Field Trips			
Bug Hunting, Animal Tracking, Bird Watching, & Shore Walking with Jim Arnosky	Jim Arnosky	HarperCollins	0688151728
National Audubon's First Field Guide: Trees	Brian Cassie	Scholastic Reference	0590054724
Girls Who Look Under Rocks: The Lives of Six Pioneering Naturalists	Jeannine Atkins	Dawn Publications	1584690119

Teaching with This Chapter

This chapter is organized into three distinct sets of activities: *Writing Basics*—activities are designed to help you extend your teaching of writing; *Poetry in Nature*—students are asked to think creatively about what they see outdoors; and *Reading About Nature*—students respond to literature selections. Handouts for all of these activities start on page 86.

My Friend, My Bud

Teaching Objectives: To review the parts of speech (nouns, adjectives, action verbs, prepositions); to use figurative language (simile or metaphor); to examine the characteristics of plants

Materials: handout, buds on cut stems or on plants outdoors, pencil, journal or notebook

Procedures and Teaching Tips: Make a survey of the school grounds for buds on trees or shrubs. If you plan to do the lesson indoors, you can prune stems with buds from your own backyard. If using stems that you cut the evening before the lesson, place them in the refrigerator overnight. Note that if the temperature indoors is warmer than the temperature outside, it may cause the buds on your cuttings to open more quickly.

Take students outdoors to find buds they wish to observe. (For the indoor version of this lesson, give each student a stem with a bud on it.) Before explaining details of the assignment, ask the students to share words that describe their buds. After getting several examples of adjectives, tell the students that they will be journalizing the experience of observing their buds. Give students copies of the handout.

Review topic sentences and how they are used to set the tone for a journal entry. Use the handout for the

first page of the journal, and staple additional pages to it. Alternatively, you can have the students use a folder or notebook for their bud journals. Encourage students to include illustrations of their buds and/or create graphs that represent how the buds changed. Wrap up the journalizing experience by displaying journals in the media center or on a bulletin board.

Extension: As an enrichment to this activity, students can report bud openings on the "Leaf Out" section of Journey North at **www.learner.org/jnorth**.

Writing About the Seasons: Signs of Fall

Teaching Objectives: To practice creating a jot list; to make predictions; to order a sequence of events; to recognize seasonal changes in nature

Materials: handout, current year calendar, clipboards if available (optional: sidewalk chalk, patio calendar or place to draw one on sidewalk)

Procedures and Teaching Tips: As students begin to work on writing skills in science, it is helpful to have them write about an occurrence that follows a natural, predictable sequence of events. This can help your students develop confidence in their skills of making predictions and writing about events in chronological order. This lesson, created for the beginning of the school year, has students writing about the progression of events in autumn.

Kinesthetic learners may benefit from the use of sidewalk chalk on a calendar patio that you have created, or on a sidewalk or unused driveway or parking lot. Moving around to make a large-scale calendar may be more effective than working with paper and pencil. If this is not available, put the

Teaching with This Chapter

handouts on clipboards and have students tour the school grounds. You can do the walkabouts several times during the course of a week or month to allow students to fill in their calendar. Because students are mainly jotting notes for this activity, it makes for excellent prewriting practice.

The Diary of a Seed

Teaching Objectives: To compare and contrast foreshadowing in literature with scientific predictions

Materials: handout, seeds, hand lenses, metric ruler, scale

Procedures and Teaching Tips: When it comes to getting your money's worth, seeds may be the best bargain a teacher can find! From harvesting seed from dried flowers—like marigolds, purple coneflowers, or sunflowers—to buying a dime package at the local dollar store, seed may literally be " a dime a dozen" or better. In Chapter 4, the activity "What Can You Learn from a Seed?" offers seedling-starter techniques for indoor use, so the students can base their writing on direct observation. Of course, for the adventurous teacher, there is the option of gardening outdoors.

In this activity, students will be learning to connect prediction in science to foreshadowing in literature as they work with 10 sentence starters. You may make up your own story starters to add to this activity. As a culminating activity, have students read their seed stories aloud, or post them on a bulletin board or school Web site. Final discussions should relate the sequence in the scientific event of a seed growing to the sequence this phenomenon created in the students' stories.

The Story of Life in a Tree

Teaching Objectives: To identify story elements, such as characters in their setting and the logical sequence events of a plot

Materials: handout, clipboards, bulletin board to post stories

Procedures and Teaching Tips: This exercise may be used as an introduction to writing fiction, or as a response to a story the class has read. Divide the students into groups by having them call out "winter, spring, summer, fall" until everyone in the class has been identified with a season. Have them form groups of four, so that all four seasons are represented in each group. Then give each group the handout so that they can see their writing assignment.

Students can decide jointly on their characters, and then each write separately about what would happen in the season they have been assigned. The students can then compare notes and work on story transitions from one season to another. They may wish to use notebook paper for a rough draft and then transfer the story to the handout.

For research, you might want to take students outdoors for observation of the current season, and then talk about the other seasons so that all students can write their parts of the story at the same time. They can also explore information on the Internet.

Teaching with This Chapter

Animal "Arti-Fact" or Fiction?

Teaching Objectives: To write original fiction short stories using a writing prompt and an artifact from nature as story starters

Materials: handout, additional writing prompts developed by teacher, feathers, snakeskin, turtle shell, leaves with caterpillar holes, other artifacts as desired, clipboard

Procedures and Teaching Tips: This is a strategy you can use indoors or outdoors, with or without artifacts. As the handout indicates, the ideal way to begin is to have students take a walk in the school yard to look for evidence of animal life. Come back to the classroom to debrief, and make a jot list as a group of what students have observed.

Ask for some ideas for first lines for a story students could write about the animal that left one of the artifacts you discovered. This will model the opening part of the story-writing process for students.

Alternatively, students may use a starter of their own from their observations, or one from the handout if they have not been inspired by nature. Another approach is to post the starters from the handout on a bulletin board. Students can each choose the one that interests them most and write it at the top of their paper. Students could then place the paper on a clipboard and go outside to continue writing while making direct observations.

The Novelization of Migration

Teaching Objectives: To practice the writing process; to use scientific facts in a work of fiction.

Materials: computer word processing software or paper and pencil, books or Internet access for research on migration

Procedures and Teaching Tips: If the activities in the chapter have been followed in sequence, students are now ready to practice the writing process. They can also include science facts in their stories. The handout provides students with a writing assignment about migration and a checklist to help them refine their drafts.

Students may ask why they are writing about migration. Migration takes place over a period of time and has a sequence of events. Just as there is a sequence to the writing process, great writing often follows a sequence of events. Hopefully, there are future writers among your students, but in the case of those who need guidance, the scientific facts about an animal's migration will give them clear ideas for writing. For instance, a right whale spends the summer off the New England coast, but comes to the coast of the Southeast in the winter to deliver its calf in warmer waters. This gives the student the setting for the story, as well as some basic plot elements to get him or her started. Guide students toward following the logical sequence of events that are found in the facts they find, and help them apply the steps from prewriting to publishing.

Teaching with This Chapter

Poetry in the Great Outdoors

Teaching Objectives: To recognize examples of acrostic poetry; to write original acrostic poems based on topics in nature

Materials: pencil, paper, handouts, clipboards, insects in a container (optional)

Procedures and Teaching Tips: Read aloud the examples on the handout of acrostic poems using *bugs* and *insects*. Ask students to think about other insect names and nature-related words while you are reading. You may want to have some insects housed temporarily in a container for inspiration, or you can take your students on a schoolyard walk to look for insects. You can almost always find ants, even if you are surrounded by concrete, and grasshoppers and beetles are usually plentiful if your school has a grass field for recess.

Extensions: After the students have practiced  acrostics with shorter words like *bugs* and *insects*, they should be ready to tackle longer words such as *caterpillar* and *butterfly*. You may want students to use their acrostic handout from this activity as a reference when writing longer acrostics. This time invite students to use *caterpillar* or *butterfly*, or another longer word of their choosing. As an added feature, require three to five facts be incorporated into the poem. Students will have to do research to find these facts. Another option would be to provide a short list of science vocabulary words, which are to be used in each poem. For instance, for a poem on caterpillars, students could use words

such as *larva*, *molting*, *life cycle*, etc. Vocabulary for the butterfly poem may include *chrysalis*, *pupa*, *nectar*, and *camouflage*. Make sure students use those words in their poems in a way that demonstrates they understand the definitions. When students are ready to publish the poems, you may wish to have them write it on paper cut in the shape of its subject.

Listening to a Story About Wetland Ecosystems

Teaching Objectives: To identify common wetlands (ponds, rivers, streams, lakes, swamp, etc.) and the animals and plants they support; to have students listen closely to a story read aloud

Materials: book on wetlands, handout

Procedures and Teaching Tips: A book such as *Salamander Rain* by Kristin Joy Serafini-Pratt helps students to learn about the animals that live in ponds and other wetland areas. Read the story aloud and show the illustrations to students. Allow them to use the handout as you are reading to record their impressions and facts from the book.

Another way to utilize a book such as this would be to put it in a reading center in the classroom, and have students complete the handout after reading it silently or in cooperative pairs.

If you have an outdoor classroom or another suitable area on the school grounds, think about creating a bog garden that is home to plants that love moisture (pitcher plants, venus fly trap, etc.) after you finish this assignment.

Teaching with This Chapter

Learning About Caterpillars and Butterflies

Teaching Objectives: To identify and order the stages of life for a butterfly; to have students listen closely to a story.

Materials: book, handout, caterpillars to raise in the classroom (optional)

Procedures and Teaching Tips: Identify prior knowledge of students by having them tell you or write down what they know about the life cycle of a butterfly. Read the book to the class, or have students read multiple copies or even various titles.

Students may complete the handout while listening to or reading the book, or they can work on the handout afterwards to strengthen their memory skills and listening skills.

Consider having live caterpillars in the classroom while you are reading about the life cycle of butterflies. Students can compare and contrast the events in the book to those with the classroom caterpillars. If your school has a butterfly garden, take the students outdoors to identify plants that attract butterflies and caterpillars. If you don't have an outdoor classroom established, identify plants from the book and think about planting some in a flowerpot to place outside near your classroom windows.

Solving an Ecological Mystery

Teaching Objectives: To identify cause and effect in literature and in nature

Materials: book, handout, newspapers

Procedures and Teaching Tips: This lesson is inspired by the book *Who Killed Cock Robin?* by Jean Craighead George, but may be used with any book that presents an ecological mystery. Have students read chapters of the book in cooperative pairs or individually for homework. You may also choose to read the book out loud over a period of time. Students should have the handout available to them before you begin reading the book, so that they can record answers to the questions as you read.

Students may participate in class discussions or even a debate about the possible causes of ecological problems. You may also want to have your students use newspapers to identify local problems in the environment that could lead to situations such as those in the book they are reading. You may wish to have your students list their predictions for the conclusion of the story on chart paper. Then the class can refer to the chart after reading the book to check for the accuracy of their predictions. Use this discussion as a springboard to talk about the reasons behind what has taken place in the plot.

Teaching with This Chapter

A Migration Story

Teaching Objectives: To identify the sequence of events in a story and the sequence of events in migration; to have students listen closely to a story

Materials: book, handout, video (optional) and Internet access (optional)

Procedures and Teaching Tips: Inspired by the book and movie, *Fly Away Home*, this lesson helps students identify the sequence of events in nature and literature. In the life of birds, imprinting, learning to fly, and following parents on the journey are often the sequence of events in migration. Students may use the Internet to compare and contrast the migration of other animals to one another.

Give students the handout before you begin the reading of your selected book. If you choose to read the book version of *Fly Away Home* to your students, you may decide to watch the video (or some video excerpts) of the movie after you've finished the book. Make sure to preview the movie and determine if it meets your school system guidelines. Students may even decide to research the real girl behind the story in the movie. Students should take notes from the book and/or movie and compare the sequence of events in literature to those necessary for successful migration in nature.

Reading from Nature Journals

Teaching Objectives: To identify ways in which setting can inspire the written word; to keep a nature journal for several days; to have students listen closely to a story

Materials: book, student journals

Procedures and Teaching Tips: Collect some of the writing of John Muir, one of the foremost authors of nature journals. Read aloud some selections to your class, or have them read selections on their own. After having completed several of the assignments in this section, students should be ready to keep a nature journal, complete with descriptive language and sketches. If possible, take students outdoors regularly for a period of several days or assign outdoor observation as homework. If it is not possible to go outdoors regularly as students work on their journals, have student observe out a window, or simply imagine what they would see outdoors. Ask students to read a selection from their own journal aloud to a partner, and ask the partner to illustrate the description of the outdoors.

If you have students keep a journal as part of your regular school-year assignments, consider giving them the option of making it a nature journal based on this activity, and have them keep it for the rest of the school year.

My Friend, My Bud

In the wintertime, trees and shrubs that have lost their leaves form *buds.* Buds are protective shells from which leaves or flowers will emerge in spring. Depending on your location, these buds become noticeable in late winter or early spring.

Directions: Find a bud outdoors and become acquainted with it, just like a new friend! Tie a piece of colorful string around the branch to mark the bud you will be watching. You are going to spend time with your new bud, and write about it in journal-style entries.

Materials: notebook for science journal, pencil, magnifying lense, and markers

Day 1—Examine your bud very carefully without touching it. Think about color, size, texture, shape, and any other features you can observe. Write a short paragraph in your journal: *My bud looks like . . . .* Use five or more adjectives to describe your bud.

Note: It may take from a week to a month for your bud to open. If you are looking at one outdoors, the weather will play a major factor. Decide with your teacher if your "Bud Journal" will be daily, weekly, or three times a week. Use the ideas below to help you create entries in your journal. Remember to start each entry with a *topic sentence*, a sentence that tells a reader of the general idea of a paragraph you are writing.

Ideas for Journal Entries

Entry 2—Write about the reaction of your bud to its new surroundings. Use two or three action verbs (Example: When the wind *blows,* my bud *bends*!)

Entry 3—Tell about your bud's neighbors—objects or animals nearby. Use nouns for this entry and underline them. Be sure to include adjectives. (Example: A small, yellow and black <u>bird</u> landed on my bud.)

Entry 4—Describe the weather conditions in your bud's environment, underlining all prepositions. (Example: My bud sways <u>in</u> the gentle breeze.)

Entry 5—Describe changes in your bud since your first entry. Use figurative language such as similes and metaphors. (Example: My bud grew as fast as my little brother!)

CD-104107 *Outdoor Science Classroom*

Name: _____ Date: _____

Writing About the Seasons: Signs of Fall

Directions: What happens to the world around you when summer ends and fall begins? Make a list of 10 changes in the world around you that fall could bring. Write down the date you think you will see it. (Think of sights, sounds, smells, what animals do, etc.) This is your *prediction*.

1. *The amount of daylight is less.   10/3/06*
2. _____
3. _____
4. _____
5. _____

6. _____
7. _____
8. _____
9. _____
10. _____

Use the calendar below to mark the actual date that each event happened on your list. Match the actual date to your prediction. If you have a calendar patio at your school, mark the events on the patio with chalk.

Sunday	Monday	Tuesday	Wednesday	Thursday	Friday	Saturday

CD-104107 *Outdoor Science Classroom*

The Diary of a Seed

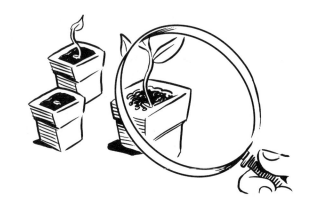

Directions: Think about what life would be like as a seed. Planting a seed can be an exciting adventure. To keep things interesting, plant one or two seeds without reading the package. Keep a journal about your seed for 10 days. The sentence starters on this page will help you get started each day.

Materials: seeds, potting soil, container, water, and notebook for journal

Day-by-Day Sentence Starters for Seeds

Day 1: *Today I was given to my new owner, _____, who thinks I am . . .*

Day 2: *After 24 hours, water has changed me by . . .*

Day 3: *Three adjectives that describe my new looks are . . .*

Day 4: *I predict that I am a _____ seed because . . .*

Day 5: *I think I will have _____ leaves and _____ flowers.*

Day 6: *My roots are_____ and my stem is . . .*

Day 7: *As a plant, my purpose in life is to . . .*

Day 8: *Compared to my original seed, I am . . .*

Day 9: *Growing seems so slow because . . .*

Day 10: *I knew water would help me grow, but I am surprised that . . .*

Use these 10 sentence starters and then add more if you continue journalizing for a long period of time. For example, you can compare your plants' growth to that of a human or of a wild animal. You can also look back. Maybe every fifth day you can compare what your plant is like now to how it looked five days ago. Be creative!

Name: _____   Date: _____

The Story of Life in a Tree

A tree is home to many animals and sometimes even other plants. Birds, squirrels, insects, and other animals live in trees, as do moss, lichens, and ferns. You are going to draw a large tree shape on paper and then write a story about what happens to all of the living things in a tree.

Directions: Choose a season. Now form a group with three other students that have chosen the other three seasons. Decide as a group which characters live in a specific tree. Fill in the blanks below. Then write about what the characters are doing during your chosen season on the back of this paper. Get back together with your group to write the whole year's story on a large sheet of paper. First, draw an outline of the chosen tree. Divide the tree into four equal sections. Label each section with the name of a season. Take turns writing your story on top of the tree shape.

Materials: large sheet of paper, water-based markers, and pencil

Characters:

Animals	Plants
_____	_____
_____	_____
_____	_____

Setting (My Season): _____

The type of tree: _____

The part of the tree: _____

Events in the plot:

_____

_____

CD-104107 *Outdoor Science Classroom*

Animal "Arti-Fact" or Fiction?

Directions: Go outdoors with your teacher. Look for animal *artifacts* on the school grounds. Some things you might find are an eggshell that fell from a bird's nest, skin shed by a snake or lizard, an anthill, droppings from a rabbit, deer tracks, leaves that have been chewed by a caterpillar, or the slimy trail of a slug or snail.

Choose one artifact and identify the animal that left it behind. Write a story about of what happened to lead up to the artifact being left there. Also imagine what may have happened to the animal afterwards as you write your story. Everyone has probably seen a movie or read a book that had animals in it. Think about those stories, and what might really happen in nature to the animal and artifact you have chosen. The writing prompts below may help you get started. Use one of these if it applies to an artifact you have seen.

Examples of Story Starters/Topic Sentences:

- *The slimy trail left across the log was left after a young snail moved slowly along, as his shell got heavier.*

- *The soft, downy feather was the last baby feather shed by the gosling, who was now officially a Canada goose.*

- *The jerking blue tail was not a sign that the skink had been killed, but a sign that his detachment defense had worked against the big snake.*

- *The empty cocoon still appeared peaceful, although no one knew if the luna moth had survived.*

- *The birds were chirping happily in the trees. They enjoyed their meal from the now-empty feeder, which had been filled only yesterday.*

- *The squirrel lying in the parking lot had left behind three babies in her pine-tree nest. How would the babies survive without their mother?*

CD-104107 *Outdoor Science Classroom*

The Novelization of Migration

Directions: Why do animals migrate? Do different animals migrate for different reasons? Using the Web site **www.learner.org/jnorth**, newspaper articles, magazines, or books, find out which animals migrate. Choose the animal that most interests you. Put yourself in your animal's place. Imagine that it is time for you to migrate. Then write a fictional account of what happens to the animal on its migration. Base your story on scientific fact. Use the guidelines below to help you tell your animal's story. Your teacher will let you know how many paragraphs your story should be.

Writing Checklist

Prewriting

- ☐ Make a "jot list" of important facts about your animal and its migration. For example, find out its migration routes, life span, food sources, and more.
- ☐ Draw a story web or use another graphic organizer to put your thoughts in order.

Outline

- ☐ Write an outline that "maps" your story, just like your animal must map its migration.

Rough Draft

- ☐ Decide whether to tell your story in first person (I, me, mine, we) or third person (he, she, they).
- ☐ Remember to include scientific facts from your jot list in your story.

Proofreading

- ☐ Check for grammar and spelling. Spell checking on a computer is not foolproof, so be sure to use a dictionary, too.
- ☐ Count the scientific facts in your story. How many did you include? _____
- ☐ Check to make sure your story has beginning, a middle, a climax, and an ending.

Final Draft and Publishing

- ☐ After your story is corrected and polished, put it in final form.
- ☐ Draw at least one picture to illustrate your story.

Name: _____   Date: _____

Poetry in the Great Outdoors

Directions: One of the easiest types of poems to write is an *acrostic poem*. That is a poem with beginning letters on each line that spell a word. The word is the subject of the poem. Look at the BUGS poem, and then change the words and write your own poem about bugs. Look around the school grounds and find out what's bugging you in the insect world. Then write your poem!

Beetles are everywhere,   **B** _____

Under rocks and in the air,   **U** _____

Going here and going there.   **G** _____

Sometimes I just stop and stare. **S** _____

Poems do not have to rhyme. Most of the time, acrostic poems don't rhyme. Now that you have written one bug poem, it shouldn't bug you to write another! This time, make it a little longer. Read the example, INSECTS. Then write your own poem in the space below.

I see insects all the time.

No, I am not scared of them.

So I try to go about my business,

Even when they get in my way,

Carrying my thoughts outside with them.

They must be happy in their carefree world,

So I get out of their way and let them be.

I _____

N _____

S _____

E _____

C _____

T _____

S _____

CD-104107 *Outdoor Science Classroom*

Listening to a Story
About Wetland Ecosystems

Directions: Listen carefully as your teacher reads from a book about a *wetland ecosystem*. Record what you hear and think about what you might see (animals and plants). Make notes on this page.

1. What are some sounds you might hear in this wetland area?

   _____   _____

2. What are some different ways animals in this wetland move about?

   _____   _____   _____

3. What are the plants like in the area? Describe one or two of them.

   _____

   _____

4. Think of a place like this one in the story that you have seen yourself. How are they alike? How are they different?

   _____

   _____

5. Choose one of these activities: a) sketch a scene from the book, or b) draw a bird's eye view of the wetland (like a map) and label the different areas. Use the space below.

Learning About Caterpillars and Butterflies

Directions: Look carefully at the book about caterpillars and butterflies. Think about how these insects change. Then fill in the blanks.

1. What does the caterpillar look like? Write three words to describe it.

_____   _____   _____

2. How does the caterpillar change during its life? Write a complete sentence that tells about the change.

_____

_____

3. Caterpillars eat leaves and butterflies drink nectar from flowers. How does this help them stay alive?

_____

4. Draw the stages of the butterfly life cycle. Label the stages: egg, caterpillar, chrysalis, and adult. Include arrows if that helps you.

1

2

3

4

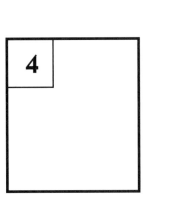

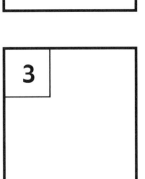

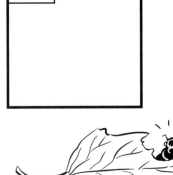

CD-104107 *Outdoor Science Classroom*

Solving an Ecological Mystery

Directions: Listen for clues in the mystery story that your teacher has chosen. Then think of the mysteries in the plot. What do you think will happen next?

1. List five important pieces of background information that are important.

_____

_____

_____

_____

_____

2. What is the main problem or mystery in the story?

_____

_____

3. Who are the main characters? Are they good guys, bad guys, suspects, victims, or innocent bystanders? Write each character's name and category. Add a second category if you need more than one to describe the character.

Character's name	Category
(example) Frog	Victim

4. Listen to enough of the story to make a guess about the solution. Then draw a map, flow chart, or story web that shows what you think happened, and how the mystery will be solved.

5. Listen to or read the rest of the story. Was your guess right?   Yes   No

CD-104107 *Outdoor Science Classroom*

A Migration Story

Directions: Think about the scientific facts about the animal(s) in the story that your teacher has chosen. Then answer these questions as you learn more about migration.

1. Why does the animal in the story migrate?

_____

_____

2. What are the advantages and disadvantages about migration?

Advantages	Disadvantages
(example) warmer weather	*Long distance travel*

3. Draw a map below that shows the route you think the animals in the story will take. Use a dotted line in pencil for your guess, or *prediction*. As you listen to more of the story, use a red crayon or pen to show what route they really took in the story.

4. Research this topic: How does this animal's migration compare to other animals? What do they have in common? What are their differences? Write your report on another sheet of paper.

     CD-104107 *Outdoor Science Classroom*